MINNESOTA VIKINGS
TRIVIA

By
Richard C. Smith

Quinlan Press
Boston

Copyright © 1988
by Richard C. Smith

All rights reserved,
including the right of reproduction
in whole or in part in any form.
Published by Quinlan Press
131 Beverly Street
Boston, MA 02114

Library of Congress Catalog
Card Number 88-42937
ISBN 1-55770-084-2

Cover design by NFL Properties, Inc.
Cover photograph by Tony Tomsic
All interior photographs courtesy of
the St. Paul Dispatch/Pioneer Press

Printed in the United States of America, 1988

I would like to thank Dan Endy with the Minnesota Vikings; the Viking alumni who contributed their memorable moments; the *St. Paul Press*; the Minnesota Historical Society; Gerry Dorner for his help in photograph selection; Scott Grams for his in-depth statistical analysis; and Maggie Stedman for her encouragement and editorial support.

Richard Currie Smith grew up on the outskirts of Sioux City, Iowa, listening to the Vikings on WNAX Radio out of Yankton, South Dakota. After graduating from Briar Cliff College in Sioux City he moved to Minneapolis-St. Paul and attended the University of Minnesota, where he earned an M.A. He works as a marketing consultant and free-lance writer.

In memory of Jack Stedman (1920-1984), a Vikings fan through and through, who now cheers on the Vikes from the upper deck.

CONTENTS

Offensive Players
    Questions 1
    Answers 13

Defensive Players
    Questions 21
    Answers 31

Special Teams
    Questions 37
    Answers 45

Coaching and Management
    Questions 49
    Answers 57

Draft and Trades
    Questions 63
    Answers 71

Photos
    Questions 75
    Answers 99

Miscellaneous
    Questions 103
    Answers 111

Team Records
    Questions 117
    Answers 129

Postseason
    Questions 135
    Answers 159

Memorable Moments
    Questiions.................... 173
    Answers 181

Offensive Players Questions

1. Who led the Vikings in touchdown receptions in their first year of play? His single-season mark of 11 is still high for the team.

2. Who was the Vikings' MVP in their first season?

3. What NFL team gave Grady Alderman to the Vikings?

4. Who was the starting quarterback in the Vikings' first regular-season game?

Offensive Players—Questions

5. What did running backs Ray Hayes and Mel Triplett each do in 1961 to put themselves in the Vikings' record book?

6. Who caught the Vikings' first touchdown pass? It was a 14-yard reception thrown by Fran Tarkenton.

7. Who led the Vikings in rushing yardage their first season?

8. Who was the first Vikings player to be selected all-pro?

9. In what year was he chosen?

10. What Vikings wide receiver was the NFL rookie of the year in 1963?

11. What is the name of the East Coast school Vikings offensive guard Dave O'Brien and 1984 Heisman Trophy winner Doug Flutie both attended?

12. In 1963, what Viking tied the all-time NFL record for the most personal fumbles recovered in a season?

13. How many of his own fumbles did he recover in 1963

14. In 1963, Fran Tarkenton was injured and did not play the final game of the season against Philadelphia. Who took over at quarterback?

Offensive Players—Questions

15. What running back leads the Vikings in career rushing attempts?

16. What four players have scored the Vikings' single-game high of three rushing touchdowns?

17. What Vikings running back was known as "The King"?

18. In 1964, the entire Vikings backfield was selected to play in the Pro Bowl. Who were these three players?

19. Two Vikings offensive linemen were also Pro Bowl selections in 1964. Can you name them?

20. What was Ahmad Rashad's given name?

21. Who has scored the most career touchdowns as a Viking?

22. At Metropolitan Stadium, in 1969, with then U.S. Vice President Spiro T. Agnew in attendance, what Viking tied the NFL record for touchdown passes in a single game?

23. How many touchdown passes did he throw that day?

24. Agnew was disappointed with his hometown team's performance against the Vikings. Who was the team that Agnew hoped would win?

Offensive Players—Questions

25. What number did Paul Flatley wear on his Jersey?

26. In 1966, what three Vikings offensive linemen started in the Pro Bowl?

27. Which of 1966 Viking Pro Bowl offensive linemen was the captain of the 1963 University of Minnesota football team?

28. In 1967, Bud Grant praised a Vikings running back saying "he has the ability to turn a five-yard run into a fifty yard run...he can explode." Who was this 1967 first-round draft choice of the Vikings who Grant liked so much?

29. What Viking is second in all-time NFL consecutive games played with 240?

30. What number did tackle Grady Alderman wear?

31. On the list of the top ten career Viking passers where does Joe Kapp stand in terms of pass-completion percentage?

32. Who are the only two Vikings players to each rush for over 100 yards in the same game?

33. What player was the Vikings' MVP in 1966 and 1968?

Offensive Players—Questions

34. Who caught the most passes for the Vikings in 1968, 1969, and 1970?

35. Who ran 80 yards for a touchdown against the Chicago Bears on November 2, 1969, setting the Vikings' record for the longest rushing touchdown?

36. After winning the NFL arm-wrestling contest in the early 1970s, what Vikings offensive lineman was considered by many the strongest man in pro football?

37. In 1971, what Vikings player led the team in pass receptions?

38. Who gained the most rushing yardage for the Vikings in 1972?

39. Who led the Vikings in passing yards in 1971?

40. How many yards did he pass for in the season?
    a) 842
    b) 1478
    c) 1737
    d) 2109

41. What running back from Cando, North Dakota, was known as the "Cando Flash"? He is third in all-time rushing attempts for the Vikings.

42. Who led the 1971 Vikings in rushing yardage?

Offensive Players—Questions

43. What Viking won the 1000 Yard Club Award as the best blocker in the NFL in 1975?

44. Who was the NFL rookie of the year in 1973?

45. What Vikings player ran for 179 yards in a single game to put himself in second place on the list of best Vikings rushing performances?

46. How many successive seasons did Chuck Foreman lead the Vikings in rushing yardage in the 1970s?

47. In what season did Chuck Foreman set the Vikings' record for consecutive 100-yard games with five?

48. What player started at running back for the Vikings in 1976 and 1977 before losing his starting position to Richey Young in 1978?

49. Who is the only Viking to rush for 200 yards in a single game?

50. Against what team did he rush for this Viking record of 200 yards on October 24, 1976?

51. In 1982, Ted Brown led the Vikings in pass receptions. It was the fewest receptions ever by the single-season leader.

Offensive Players—Questions

How many balls did he catch for the Vikings that year?

52. What is tight end Steve Jordan's Jersey number?

53. With just over two minutes to go in a December 4, 1977 game, Tommy Kramer came in and established himself as the Vikings' quarterback of the future. Who were the Vikings playing?

54. Who was the quarterback he came in for and replaced?

55. What did Kramer do in these last two minutes?

56. Who were the three receivers he hit for touchdowns?

57. What was the final score?

58. Against Buffalo on December 16, 1979, Tommy Kramer threw, what was at that time, the second-highest number of passes in a single game in NFL history. How many passes did Kramer throw that day?

59. Two years later Kramer moved down to third place on the all-time NFL list in passes thrown in a single game. Which Vikings player took over second place?

Offensive Players—Questions

60. Fran Tarkenton established the Vikings' record for most consecutive pass attempts without an interception. How many passes in a row did Tarkenton throw without getting one picked off?

61. In what place is Fran Tarkenton in Vikings career rushing average?

62. How many seasons did Fran Tarkenton lead the NFL in pass completions?

63. Fran Tarkenton's most productive year for touchdown passes was as a New York Giant in 1967. How many touchdown passes did he throw that year?

64. In what year did Tarkenton rush for a personal and Viking season high of five touchdowns?

65. Who tied Tarkenton for the most rushing touchdowns by a Vikings quarterback in a single season?

66. In what year did Tommy Kramer attempt a Vikings' record of 593 passes?

67. Of the 39 games in which Fran Tarkenton quarterbacked the Vikings without throwing an interception, how many did the Vikings win?

68. How many seasons did Fran Tarkenton play pro football?

Offensive Players—Questions

69. Which Vikings offensive lineman said the following: "The only way you can keep your sanity, let alone your job, when Tarkenton starts to scramble is to approach the whole thing like a World War I fighter pilot. You have to look for targets of opportunity."

70. Which Vikings player led the NFL and set a team record for average yards per catch in 1988?

71. What was Fran Tarkenton's 1962 rushing average?

72. In 1966, before Tarkenton went to the New York Giants, they were 2-12. What was their record in 1967?

73. Fran Tarkenton holds the all-time NFL record for touchdown passes. How many did he throw in his career?

74. Fran Tarkenton was inducted into the Pro Football Hall of Fame on August second of what year?

75. What former Vikings running back became a star on television's "Hill Street Blues"?

76. What Ivy League school was he drafted out of in 1972?

Offensive Players—Questions

77. Which Vikings player has the highest number of seasons leading the team in rushing yardage?

78. How many seasons did he rush for over 1,000 yards?

79. Who is the only other Viking to rush for over 1,000 yards in a season?

80. What player holds the single-game combined rushing, receiving, and return yardage mark for the Vikings?

81. How many combined yards did he total that day?

82. Who was the player Bud Grant referred to when he said, "Other quarterbacks run out of bounds; _____ turns upfield and looks for a tackle to run into"?

83. Who led the Vikings in rushing yardage in 1984? He was the top rookie rusher in the NFC.

84. Who leads the Vikings in number of seasons with 50 or more receptions?

85. How many seasons did he catch more than 50 balls?

Offensive Players—Questions

86. Who set the Vikings' single-game reception yardage mark of 210 yards?

87. What other Viking has gained over 200 yards receiving in a single game?

88. What Vikings receiver was All-Big Ten and an honorable mention All-American quarterback at the University of Iowa in 1955? He was also selected MVP in the 1956 East-West Game.

89. Who set the Vikings' single-game pass reception mark against New England in 1979?

90. How many receptions did he make that day?

91. Who leads the Vikings in number of 1,000-yard receiving seasons?

92. Who became the second Vikings wide receiver to win NFL rookie of the year honors?

93. In a game against Philadelphia on September 9, 1984, a Vikings running back threw a 20-yard touchdown pass to Tommy Kramer. Name the player who also rushed for 105 yards that day.

94. Who holds the Vikings' career receiving record with 400?

95. Who is third with 339?

Offensive Players Answers

1. Jerry Reichow, 1961

2. Hugh McElhenny

3. Green Bay. He was one of the original players donated by rival teams under the 1961 expansion agreement.

4. George Shaw

5. They were the two players in 1961 to have 100-yard rushing games for the newly formed Vikings.

6. Bob Schnelker

Offensive Players—Answers

7. Hugh McElhenny, 570 yards

8. Tommy Mason

9. 1963

10. Paul Flatley

11. Boston College

12. Running back Billy Butler

13. Eight

14. Ron VanderKelen

15. Bill Brown, 1,627

16. Tommy Mason, Clint Jones, Chuck Foreman (he scored three touchdowns on two separate occasions), and D.J. Dozier.

17. Hugh McElhenny

18. Backfield: Fran Tarkenton, Bill Brown, and Tommy Mason

19. Offensive linemen: Grady Alderman and Mick Tingelhoff

20. Bobby Moore

Offensive Players—Answers

21. Bill Brown

22. Joe Kapp

23. 7

24. The Baltimore Colts

25. 85

26. Grady Alderman, Milt Sunde, Mick Tingelhoff

27. Milt Sunde

28. Clint Jones

29. Mick Tingelhoff, 1962-78

30. 67

31. Tenth, with 50.2%

32. Tommy Mason (137 yards) and Bill Brown (103 yards) against Baltimore on September 13, 1964.

33. Bill Brown

34. Gene Washington

35. Clint Jones

36. Ed White

Offensive Players—Answers

37. Bob Grim with 45

38. Oscar Reed, 639 yards

39. Gary Cuozzo

40. a) 842, the fewest ever by a Vikings single-seasons passing yardage leader

41. Dave Osborn

42. Clint Jones with 675 yards

43. Ron Yary

44. Chuck Foreman

45. Ted Brown, against Green Bay on October 23, 1983, in a 20-17 overtime win

46. Six (1973-1978)

47. 1975

48. Brent McClanahan

49. Chuck Foreman

50. Philadelphia

51. 31

52. 83

Offensive Players—Answers

53. San Francisco

54. Bobby Lee

55. He threw three touchdown passes

56. Ahmad Rashad for 8 yards, Bob Tucker for 9, and finally Sammy White with a 69-yard bomb

57. Minnesota won 28-27

58. 61

59. Steve Dils, Minnesota vs. Tampa Bay, who threw 62 passes on this day

60. 155 in late 1977

61. First, 5.6 yards

62. Three

63. 29

64. 1961

65. Wade Wilson in 1987 with five

66. 1981

67. 31

68. 1 8

Offensive Players—Answers

69. Grady Alderman

70. Anthony Carter, 24.3-yard average

71. 8.8 yards

72. 7-7

73. 342

74. 1986

75. Ed Marinaro

76. Cornell.

77. Chuck Foreman with six

78. Three

79. Ted Brown, 1,063 yards in 1981

80. Darrin Nelson vs. Green Bay, November 13, 1983

81. 278 (119 rushing, 137 receiving, and 22 returning)

82. Joe Kapp

83. Alfred Anderson, 773 yards

Offensive Players—Answers

84. Ahmad Rashad

85. Six, 1976-81

86. Sammy White vs. Detroit, November 7, 1976

87. Paul Flatley

88. Jerry Reichow

89. Rickey Young

90. 15

91. Ahmad Rashad, two, 1979-80

92. Sammy White in 1976

93. Alfred Anderson

94. Ahmad Rashad

95. Ted Brown

Defensive Players Questions

1. Which Vikings player shares the NFL record for safeties in a single season?

2. Who led the Vikings in interceptions in his first year of play with five?

3. Which outside linebacker took over at middle linebacker for the Vikings when Rip Hawkins retired during the 1966 training camp?

4. Who leads the Vikings in career interceptions with 53?

Defensive Players—Questions

5. With 51 interceptions, who is in second place?

6. Which Vikings defensive tackle was knows as "The Philosopher" because of his love of poetry and his quiet demeanor off the field?

7. In 1963, what Viking set the all-time NFL record for fumble recoveries in a single season?

8. Who owns the all-time NFL record for the most career fumbles recovered?

9. Which Viking is third on the all-time NFL Fumble-Recovery list beind Dick Butkus?

10. Which two Vikings players are tied for the team lead in number of seasons with the most pass interceptions? They each have led Minnesota in this category four times.

11. Who intercepted the most passes as a Viking in a single season?

12. How many interceptions did he have when he established the team record in 1975?

Defensive Players—Questions

13. What two Vikings players are tied for second place in single-season interceptions?

14. Which Vikings defensive back was nicknamed "the Hacker"?

15. In 1971, who intercepted the most passes for the Vikings?

16. Who was the first rookie to make the NFL all-pro team?

17. What year did he win this honor?

18. He led the league in interceptions that year. How many interceptions did he make?

19. Paul Krause joined the Vikings in what year?

20. Which defensive back, who was a "walk-on" in 1965, by 1966 had won a starting position in the Vikings secondary? He played for the team through 1969.

21. Who made 97 assisted tackles in a single season to set the Vikings' record?

22. The Vikings' record for consecutive games with an interception is held by Paul Krause. In how many games in a row did he pick off a pass?

Defensive Players—Questions

23. Which five Vikings defensive linemen were the anchor of the tough 1969 "Purple People Eater" defense?

24. Which player was the only Viking to make all-pro in 1980?

25. What was the jersey number of Alan Page?

26. Which Viking was a four-time NFC defensive player of the year?

27. Which Vikings player has the most career solo tackles and total tackles?

28. In 1971, the Vikings' single-season interception return yardage record was set by what player?

29. In a game against Chicago that year he also set the Vikings' mark for the longest interception return. How many yards did he return the ball?

30. Who is second to Paul Krause in career interception return yardage for the Vikings?

31. Who holds the Vikings' career record for sacks?

Defensive Players—Questions

32. The Vikings' longest return of an opponent's fumble occurred in 1961 covering 88 yards. Who recovered the ball and ran it back for a touchdown to set the Vikings' record?

33. Head coach Norm Van Brocklin gave a player the nickname "Hunkie," which meant someone lacking in intelligence, supposedly to make the player angry because Van Brocklin felt he played better when he was mad. Name the defensive back who got angry at first but then came to embrace the name as his own?

34. Jim Marshall wore what number?

35. Alan Page was picked in the first round in 1967 out of what university?

36. What Viking is third on the NFL's all-time list for the most seasons played?

37. Name the player who was born in Superior Wisconsin, attended Superior State College, and later became a starter in the Vikings' defensive line in 1974.

38. Who was the NFL lineman of the year in 1973?

39. What was Vikings linebacker Roy Winston's nickname?

Defensive Players—Questions

40. What Viking holds third place in the NFL record books for the most opponent fumbles recovered in a season with seven?

41. What Vikings defensive back was an all-big Ten selection as a junior and senior along with being captain of the 1970 Minnesota Gophers football team?

42. What Viking from Flint, Michigan was an all-state football and basketball player as well as a top major league baseball prospect during his high school years?

43. Where did he play his college ball from 1960-63?

44. Who was the head coach he played under in college from 1961-63?

45. This player was chosen co-captain of the university football team. With what other Viking did he share the honor?

46. The NFL record for consecutive games played is held by which Viking?

47. What is the all-time consecutive-game record that he holds?

48. Who is second behind Carl Eller in quarterback sacks for the Vikings?

Defensive Players—Questions

49. Who made the most sacks for the Vikings in a single season?

50. Who became the Vikings' starting right linebacker in 1977?

51. While at UCLA, he played against his brother, Rod. What school did Rod play for?

52. Who made five sacks in a single game to set the Vikings' record?

53. Name the four Vikings who are tied for second place in single-game sacks with four each.

54. What Stanford All-American became the Vikings' regular middle linebacker when Lonnie Warwick was injured?

55. After replacing Warwick, how many times did he play in the Pro Bowl?

56. Who made the most solo tackles during a season as a Viking?

57. Who was "Moose"?

58. What Vikings player made the most solo tackles in a single game? He had 16.

59. Who made 15 in a game against Chicago on October 27, 1985?

Defensive Players—Questions

60. Nine players share the NFL record for the most opponents' fumbles recovered in a single game. Who recovered three for the Vikings in one game to join this group?

61. Who was "Bench Warmer Bob"?

62. Who leads the Vikings in career assisted tackles?

63. Whose nickname was "Duck"?

64. In a game against the New Orleans Saints on November 15, 1981, what player made a team-record 11 assisted tackles? Scott Studwell would tie him with the same number in a game two years later.

65. Against Detroit on November 17, 1985, Scott Studwell set the team record for total tackles. How many tackles did he make that day?

66. In what season did Scott Studwell set the team record for total tackles?

67. How many tackles did he make that year?

68. What Vikings' Pro-Bowl selection in 1969 and 1970 came to the team in a trade with the Rams for Jack Snow in 1965?

Defensive Players—Questions

69. Defensive tackle Gary Larsen came from what Minnesota Division III private school?

70. Who spent his first three years as a Viking substituting for Jim Marshall and Carl Eller? He ended up taking over Eller's former spot when Carl retired.

71. When Alan Page was waived in 1978, who took over his spot in the defensive line?

72. Who had the most solo tackles of any Vikings defensive lineman in 1979?

73. Defensive back Karl Kassulke came out of what Iowa private university in 1963?

74. What Vikings defensive lineman won all-pro honors in 1982?

75. Matt Blair is out of what Big Eight University?

76. Who broke the University of Illinois single-season record for number of tackles which was previously held by Dick Butkus?

77. Who led the Vikings in pass interceptions in 1984?

Defensive Players—Questions

78. After a difficult but highly successful transition from linebacker to defensive end, what Vikings' first-round draft pick said, "If you're a middle-round pick and you go out and start, you're destined to be a star. If you're a first-round pick and don't get on the field right away, people automatically question your ability."

79. The Vikings' answer to the Bears' refrigerator was Tim Newton. By what nickname was he known?

80. Who led the 1985 Vikings in interceptions by picking off five passes?

81. Who led the Vikings in sacks and sack yardage in 1985?

82. In 1985, for the first time in Vikings history, two rookies made over 100 total tackles each. Who were these two rookie players?

83. What player led the Vikings in sacks in 1987? His total of 11 was fourth in the NFC.

84. Name the Vikings three defensive players who were selected to the Pro Bowl after the 1987 season.

85. Name the Vikings rookie defensive tackle who came in and started all season in 1987.

Defensive Players Answers

1. Alan Page, who had two in 1971.

2. Rip Hawkins

3. Lonnie Warwick

4. Paul Krause

5. Bobby Bryant

6. Defensive tackle Paul Dickson, 1961-70

7. Don Hultz. He recovered nine fumbles and all of them were opponents' fumbles.

Defensive Players—Answers

8. Jim Marshall, 29

9. Carl Eller with 23

10. Ed Sharockman and Bobby Bryant

11. Paul Krause

12. 10 interceptions

13. Bobby Bryant, in 1969, and Issiac Holt, in 1986. Both had eight.

14. Dale Hackbart

15. Defensive back Charlie West had seven interceptions to lead the team.

16. Future Viking Paul Krause, when he played for the Washington Redskins

17. 1964

18. 12

19. 1968

20. Earsell Mackbee

21. Scott Studwell, 1985

22. Six

Defensive Players—Answers

23. Carl Eller, Paul Dickson, Alan Page, Gary Larsen, Jim Marshall (Eller, Page, Larsen, and Marshall were the four starters.)

24. Matt Blair

25. 88

26. Alan Page

27. Scott Studwell. He was 1,060 solo tackles and 1,579 total tackles.

28. Charley West, 236 yards

29. 89 yards

30. Ed Sharockman

31. Carl Eller, 134.

32. Ed Sharockman

33. Karl Kassulke

34. 70

35. Notre Dame

36. Jim Marshall, 20

37. Doug Sutherland

Defensive Players—Answers

38. Alan Page

39. "Mooney"

40. Alan Page. He did it in 1970.

41. Jeff Wright

42. Paul Krause. He turned down a large bonus from the major leagues to attend college.

43. The University of Iowa

44. Jerry Burns

45. Wally Hilgenberg

46. Jim Marshall

47. 282 games, 1960-79

48. Jim Marshall, 132½

49. Alan Page, 19 in 1976

50. Fred McNeill

51. USC

52. Randy Holloway, vs. Atlanta, September 16, 1984

53. Jim Marshall, Gary Larsen, Alan Page, and Doug Martin

Defensive Players—Answers

54. Jeff Siemon, in 1972

55. Four

56. Jeff Siemon, 170 tackles in 1978

57. Carl Eller

58. Scott Studwell, vs. San Francisco in 1984 and Detroit in 1985

59. Joey Browner

60. Joey Browner, vs. San Francisco, September 8, 1985

61. Bob Lurtsema

62. Scott Studwell with 519

63. Defensive tackle James White

64. Matt Blair

65. 24

66. 1981

67. 230

68. Gary Larsen

69. Concordia College, in St. Paul, Minnesota

70. Mark Mullaney

Defensive Players—Answers

71. James White

72. James White, 63

73. Drake

74. Doug Martin

75. Iowa State, 1974

76. Scott Studwell

77. Rufus Bess with three

78. Chris Doleman, the Vikings' 1985 first-round pick

79. "Icebox"

80. John Turner

81. Keith Millard. His 11 sacks for a 64½ yards was more than double that of any other Viking.

82. Chris Doleman (113 total tackles) and Tim Newton (106)

83. Chris Doleman

84. Joey Browner, Chris Doleman, Scott Studwell

85. Henry Thomas

Special Teams Questions

1. What former Vikings kicker was a starting running back at the University of Pittsburgh?

2. Who was the last Viking to return a punt for a touchdown in the regular season?

3. What number did Rick Danmeier wear on his jersey?

4. Exactly 11 years apart, two players set and tied the Vikings' record for the most field goals made in a single game. Who were these two great kickers?

Special Teams—Questions

5. How many field goals did they each make?

6. Fred Cox holds the NFL record for the most consecutive games scoring field goals. In how many successive games did he make one or more field goals?

7. How many years did Cox play for the Vikings?

8. What Vikings kicker, born in St. Paul, Minnesota, played for the 1969 and 1970 Suburban Conference champion, White Bear Lake (Minn.) High School?

9. Who holds the Vikings' record for most punts returned in a season?

10. Who punted for the Vikings in 1963?

11. In what seasons did Mike Eischeid handle the punting chores for the Vikings?

12. Who did the punting for the Vikings in 1975, 1976, 1977?

13. Who holds the record for the longest Vikings' field goal?

14. How many yards was this record-setting field goal?

Special Teams—Questions

15. What jersey number did Jan Stenerud wear as a Viking?

16. In 1985, one Viking was chosen for the Pro Bowl. Which special teams player attained this honor?

17. After Fred Cox, who has kicked the most field goals as a Viking in a single season?

18. What outstanding defensive back was a holder for Fred Cox?

19. Who is second in career field goals made by a Viking with 70?

20. How many field goals is he behind Vikings leader Fred Cox?

    a) 24
    b) 39
    c) 147
    d) 212

21. Who led the Vikings in scoring in 1983 with 108 points?

22. Who led the Vikings in total points scored in 1962?

23. In what seasons did Jan Stenerud kick field goals for the Vikings?

24. At what South Dakota school did Rick Danmeier play his college ball?

Special Teams—Questions

25. Over how many seasons did Rick Danmeier lead the Vikings in total points scored?

26. Fred Cox, the Vikings' leader in conversions made in a single season, hit 46 in 1975. Who is second to him with only two less?

27. In what season did he kick 44 to miss going ahead of Cox by only three kicks?

28. How many points after touchdowns did Fred Cox make to set the Vikings' single-game mark?

29. Cox holds the Vikings' mark for the most consecutive points after touchdowns. How many did he kick in a row?

   a) 48
   b) 97
   c) 199
   d) 285

30. What defensive back out of St. Cloud State was chosen captain of the kicking team in 1984 after leading the Vikings in special team tackles in each of his first four seasons?

31. What Viking leads the team in career blocked kicks?

Special Teams—Questions

32. How many did he block?

33. Who is second on the Vikings in career blocked kicks?

34. The Vikings' longest blocked punt that went for a touchdown was 28 yards in a 1976 game. Who blocked this punt?

35. Name the four Vikings players who have blocked two kicks in a single game.

36. The longest punt by a Viking traveled 77 yards from the line of scrimmage. Who kicked this punt in a game against Green Bay in 1962?

37. Which punter played two seasons in the Canadian Football League before joining the Vikings in 1964? He led the NFL in punting with a 46.4 yard average in 1964.

38. Who was the Vikings punter in 1970?

39. Who leads the Vikings in punting yardage for a single game?

40. Who has the best career punting average of any Vikings kicker?

41. Who is second in career punting average for the Vikings?

Special Teams—Questions

42. Two quarterbacks have punted for the Vikings, one for a single season and the other for two seasons. Who are these two players?

43. What Vikings player has kicked more punts than the next two closest punters combined?

44. Which Vikings player has the best career punt-return average (20 or more returns) with 11.1 yards per return?

45. Who has returned the most punts for the Vikings?

46. Who set the Vikings' single-season punt return yardage record in 1981?

47. Which Viking set the all-time NFL record for kickoff-return yardage in his rookie season with 1,345?

48. In what season did he set the record?

49. Who returned a kickoff 101 yards against Baltimore in November, 1965, for the Vikings' record?

50. What two Vikings players are tied for second with kickoff returns of 99 yards each?

Special Teams—Questions

51. Two Vikings are tied for the most kickoff returns in a season. Who are they and how many did they each bring back?

52. Who owns the best Vikings' career kickoff return average?

53. Who leads the Vikings in total kickoff returns with 104?

Special Teams Answers

1. Fred Cox

2. Leo Lewis, 78 yards against Atlanta in 1987

3. 14

4. Fred Cox in 1973 and Jan Stenerud in 1984

5. Five

6. 31

7. 15, 1963-1977

Special Teams—Answers

8. Rick Danmeier

9. Kevin Miller, 48, in 1978

10. Fred Cox, for a 38.7-yard average

11. 1972-74

12. Neil Clabo

13. Jan Stenerud vs. Atlanta, September 16, 1984

14. 54 yards

15. 3

16. Joey Browner

17. Benny Ricardo, 25, in 1983

18. Paul Krause

19. Rick Danmeier

20. d) 212

21. Benny Ricardo

22. Jim Christopherson with 61 points

23. 1984 and 1985

Special Teams—Answers

24. Sioux Falls

25. Five, 1978-82

26. Chuck Nelson

27. 1986

28. Seven. (He did it twice in his career.)

29. c) 199, from September 15, 1968 to September 15, 1974

30. Keith Nord

31. Matt Blair

32. 20

33. Alan Page, with 15

34. Nate Allen

35. Alan Page, Matt Blair (he did it twice), Tim Irwin, and Neil Elshire

36. Mike Mercer

37. Bobby Walden

38. Tom McNeil

39. Greg Coleman, 489 yards against Green Bay in 1982 (12 punts)

Special Teams—Answers

40. Bobby Walden, 42.9 yards

41. King Hill, 41.0 yards

42. King Hill in 1968 and Bobby Lee in 1969 and 1971

43. Greg Coleman, 675 punting attempts

44. Leo Lewis

45. Charlie West, 123

46. Eddie Payton, 303 yards

47. Buster Rhymes

48. 1985

49. Lance Rentzel

50. Eddie Payton, in 1981 (vs. Oakland) and Clint Jones, 1967 (New York Giants)

51. Eddie Payton in 1980 and Buster Rhymes in 1985, 53 each

52. Bob Reed, 27.1

53. Eddie Payton

Coaching and Management Questions

1. Which of the original Vikings owners was for a time the president of the Minneapolis Lakers basketball team?

2. Who was the Vikings' first head coach?

3. What was the starting yearly salary for the Vikings' first head coach?

4. A highly successful Big Ten coach interviewed for the job of Vikings head coach but withdrew when the media leaked news of his visit with the Vikings. Who was the individual that nearly became the team's first head coach?

Coaching and Management—Questions

5. Coach Norm Van Brocklin had one winning season as a Viking. In what year did the team go 8-5-1 under his direction?

6. How many years was Van Brocklin the head coach of the Vikings?

7. What substitute quarterback—later picked up by the Vikings—led his team to a 41-21 win over the Vikings, prompting head coach Norm Van Brocklin to resign for one day?

8. Who was the Vikings' first general manager?

9. How much did the Vikings pay to the other NFL teams for their first season's players?

    a) $600,000
    b) $1.2 million
    c) $2.5 million
    d) $3.5 million

10. What former Vikings head coach is ninth on the all-time NFL records list for punting average?

11. Who was the Vikings' general manager before Mike Lynn?

Coaching and Management—Questions

12. Through what years did Finks hold that position?

13. Lynn's involvement with the NFL began when he sought a franchise for the city he was living in at the time. In what southeastern city did he attempt to place an NFL team? Through Lynn's efforts several NFL preseason games were held in this city.

14. Who joined the Vikings in 1967 as offensive line coach after coaching with Bud Grant in Winnipeg? He has continued in this capacity for the team for over 20 years.

15. Which Vikings head coach has French, Scottish, and American Indian ancestry?

16. Bud Grant was born on May 20 of what year?

17. What is Bud Grant's hometown?

18. What branch of the service did Bud Grant join after graduating from high school?

19. After completing his military service, where did Bud Grant attend college?

Coaching and Management—Questions

20. In Bud Grant's first day at the University, what Minneapolis sports reporter did he meet on the steps of Cooke Hall who was also on his first day at the job?

21. In what college sports did Bud Grant earn letters?

22. Bud Grant said of coach Dave Mac-Millian, "I learned more about handling people from Dave than I have from anybody else. He had respect for everybody on the team, and that was a new experience for me. I'd been used to being on teams where the best players always commanded the most respect. That wasn't Mac's way...he had as much respect for the last sub as he did for the star of the team." What coaching job did Dave MacMillian hold when he played such a significant role in Grant's life?

23. Who was Grant's football coach at the University of Minnesota?

24. What position did Grant play on the Minnesota football team?

25. What athletic awards did Grant win at the University of Minnesota?

Coaching and Management—Questions

26. When he graduated from college, what professional team did Grant join for $3,500 a year?

27. What position did he play?

28. After playing on the NBA Championship Laker team in 1949-50, Grant continued for one more season with the Lakers, then in 1951 joined another professional team. What team did Grant play for in 1951?

29. In what round of the 1950 college football draft was Grant selected?

30. While playing defensive and, Grant led the team in sacks his rookie year. What was his playing weight?

31. In 1951, Grant shifted to offensive end for the Eagles and caught a team-high 57 passes—second only to Elroy (Crazylegs) Hirsch in the entire NFL. What honor did Grant win that year?

32. Grant did not play in the Pro Bowl game. Why?

33. What did Grant do after his departure from the Eagles?

Coaching and Management—Questions

34. After many successful years coaching the Canadian team he had played for, Grant became head coach of the Vikings. What was the name of the Canadian team?

35. How old was Grant when he took over as the Bombers' head coach?

36. When Bud Grant came to the Vikings he had to adjust to a different number of players on the field. How many players had Grant been able to send on the field in Canadian Football?

37. The equivalent to the Super Bowl in Canadian Football is the Grey Cup. How many Grey Cup championships did Grant win at Winnipeg?

38. What year did Grant take over as Vikings head coach?

39. In Grant's first year as head coach, what was the Vikings' record?

40. What year was Grant's first winning season as the Vikings' head coach?

41. How many years did Grant serve as head coach of the Vikings?

Coaching and Management—Questions

42. Under Grant how many times did the Vikings make the playoffs?

43. Grant has 290 victories in professional football. How many of those were as the Vikings' head coach?

44. How many head coaches have won more professional football games than Bud Grant?

45. What Vikings defensive line coach later gained fame with the Chicago Bears for his innovative and effective defense?

46. When was he with the Vikings?

47. In what year did Mike Lynn become the Vikings' general manager?

48. What year did Ralph Kohl take over as the Vikings' head scout?

49. In what two seasons did Murray Warmath coach for the Vikings?

50. Les Steckel became head coach in what year?

51. Where did Les Steckel play his college ball?

52. What Vikings coaching position did Les Steckel have before his promotion to head coach?

Coaching and Management—Questions

53. Who joined the Vikings as defensive line coach in 1985 after being head coach at Stanford from 1980-83?

54. What highly successful head coach did Jerry Burns replace at the University of Iowa in 1961?

55. How many Super Bowls did Burns coach in as an NFL assistant coach?

56. What year did Burns join the Vikings as offensive coordinator?

57. Jerry Burns was born on January 24 of what year?

58. What year did Burns take over as Vikings head coach?

59. What position did Burns have on the Vikings' coaching staff in 1985?

60. Who became the Vikings' offensive coordinator in 1986 when Burns took over as head coach?

61. For what NFL team was he offensive coordinator before coming to the Vikings?

Coaching and Management Answers

1. Max Winter

2. Norm Van Brocklin

3. Norm Van Brocklin signed for $25,000.

4. Ara Parseghian, who coached Northwestern University at the time

5. 1964

6. Six years, 1961-66

7. Gary Cuozzo, Baltimore Colts, 1965

Coaching and Management—Answers

8. Bert Rose

9. a) $600,000

10. Norm Van Brocklin

11. Jim Finks

12. 1964-74

13. Memphis, Tennessee

14. John Michels

15. Bud Grant

16. 1927

17. Superior, Wisconsin

18. The Navy

19. The University of Minnesota

20. Sid Hartman

21. He was one of the University of Minnesota's most versatile athletes, winning nine letters, three each in football, baseball, and basketball.

22. He was the University of Minnesota basketball coach and baseball coach during Grant's early years at the university.

Coaching and Management—Answers

23. The legendary Bernie Bierman

24. End, both offensive and defensive

25. He was chosen All-Big Nine in football and most valuable player in football and basketball.

26. The Minneapolis Lakers basketball team

27. He was a 6-3 forward

28. The Philadelphia Eagles football team

29. Grant was the 1950 first-round pick of the Philadelphia Eagles.

30. 200 pounds

31. He was selected to the Pro Bowl

32. Because he refused to sign the contract the Eagles were offering him for the next season. The Eagles informed him that unless he signed he could not play in the Pro Bowl.

33. He went to the Canadian Football League where he starred for several seasons as both a defensive and offensive end.

34. The Winnipeg Blue Bombers

35. 29 years old

Coaching and Management—Answers

36. 12

37. Four

38. 1967

39. 3-8-3

40. In his second year, 1968, they were 8-6.

41. 18 years

42. 12 times

43. 168; 122 were for Winnipeg

44. Only one, the legendary Chicago Bear, George Halas, who has 325 victories

45. Buddy Ryan

46. 1976-77

47. 1975

48. 1978

49. 1978-79

50. 1984

51. Kansas, 1964-67

Coaching and Management—Answers

52. Receivers coach

53. Paul Wiggin

54. Forest Evashevski

55. Six, two with the Packers and four with the Vikings

56. 1968

57. 1927

58. 1986

59. Assistant head coach/offensive coordinator

60. Bob Schnelker

61. The Packers, from 1982-85

The Draft and Trades Questions

1. Who was the Vikings' first draft pick ever? He also was the first player chosen in 1961.

2. How big was the bonus the Vikings' first draft choice received?

3. Who was the middle linebacker the Vikings chose as their second selection in the 1961 draft?

4. What is the complete name of the Methodist minister's son who was the Viking franchise's third pick?

The Draft and Trades—Questions

5. What stand-out defensive tackle was the number-one draft choice of the Los Angeles Rams in 1959? He was acquired by the Vikings in a trade with Cleveland in 1961 and played for the Vikes through 1970.

6. Which perennial Vikings all-pro offensive lineman signed as a free agent with the team in 1962?

7. What defensive back—who played for the Vikings for 10 years—was drafted in the eleventh round by the Detroit Lions in 1963 and purchased from them by Minnesota in August of that same year?

8. What All-American from the University of California was chosen in the 1959 draft by the Washington Redskins? He played for the Vikings from 1967-1979.

9. Who was the defensive back out of South Carolina that the Vikings drafted in the seventh round of the 1967 draft?

10. Two of the Vikings' three first-round draft picks in 1967 played on the same great college team. Who were these two players?

11. What school possessed this incredible talent in 1966?

12. The Vikings had one more first round draft choice in 1967. Who did they take?

The Draft and Trades—Questions

13. Two of these first-round picks came from trades. One was with the Rams, in which the Vikes gave up an all-pro player as part of the deal. Can you name this player?

14. The other first-round pick came by trading a player who had been chosen to represent the Vikings in the 1964 and 1965 Pro Bowls. Who was this player?

15. Who was the first player selected in the NFL's 1968 college draft?

16. Chuck Foreman, who rushed for a team-record 5,879 yards, was drafted by the Vikings in 1973. What round was he drafted on?

17. Passing up his final year at Ohio State, what defensive end played for Saskatchewan of the Canadian League in 1959 and then came to the Vikings through a trade with Cleveland in 1962?

18. Who played weakside linebacker for the Vikings in their league-leading 1969 defense? He was acquired through a trade with the Lions in 1968.

19. After taking over as head coach of the Washington Redskins in 1969, who asked the poignant question, "Why did they ever trade Paul Krause off this club?"

The Draft and Trades—Questions

20. The Vikings traded their number-one pick in the 1968 college draft to New Orleans to acquire what player?

21. Who was the running back from Ohio State the Vikings chose as their first-round pick in 1971? He played for the Vikings only in the year he was drafted.

22. In what year was Ed White the Vikings' first-round draft choice?

23. Which Vikings player was the first-round draft choice of the St. Louis Cardinals in 1972? He was out of the University of Oregon.

24. What linebacker was the fourth player taken in the entire 1985 draft?

25. Who was the first defensive lineman the Vikings drafted in the first round?

26. Name the first defensive lineman the Vikings drafted in the first round who played for the Vikings.

27. What year was he drafted by the Vikings?

28. Out of what school was Carl Eller drafted? While there, he won All-American and All-Big Ten honors.

The Draft and Trades—Questions

29. Who was the defensive end from UCLA the Vikings chose in the first round in 1974?

30. The Vikings traded their second and third picks in 1980 to San Francisco in order to get an LSU defensive back in the second round of that year's draft. Who did they select?

31. What second-team All-American defensive tackle from the University of Washington was a first-round choice in the 1980 draft by the Vikings?

32. Who was the last Vikings quarterback drafted in the first round?

33. The Vikings selected a solid starter in the third round of the 1981 draft out of Tennessee. Who was this offensive lineman?

34. In 1983, the Vikings chose defensive back Joey Browner as their first-round draft pick. Where did he play his college ball?

35. Who was the defensive end the Vikings chose as their first draft choice in 1984?

36. The Vikings always have liked to draft defensive linemen in the first round. Of the club's 31 total first-round draft choices, how many have been defensive linemen?

The Draft and Trades—Questions

37. Name the Vikings' twelfth-round pick in 1986 who played second string for Florida State and is now a starter. Vikings head scout Ralph Kohl considers this player his best all-time find.

38. The Vikings acquired quarterback Rich Gannon from what AFC team on May 6, 1987?

39. In what year did the Vikings not draft a single running back, quarterback, or wide receiver?

40. In 1986, what Vikings defensive back was one of only 10 NFC players to have not been chosen in an NFL college draft who had played eight years or more in the NFL? The Vikings picked him up on waivers from Buffalo on September 9, 1982.

41. What Vikings all-pro offensive tackle's draft rights were picked up on opening day of the 1986 draft after his release from the USFL's Memphis Showboats?

42. Darrin Nelson was the Vikings' first round pick in what year?

43. Three running backs who later starred in the NFL were taken after Nelson by other teams. One of these was the Heisman Trophy winner. Who were those three running backs?

The Draft and Trades—Questions

44. The Vikings drafted a defensive back out of Marshall College in the seventh round in 1983, who was the 35th defensive back selected and the 186th player taken overall. He became a starter and by 1986 ranked third on the team in solo tackles. Who is this Viking cornerback who beat the odds?

45. What wide receiver did the Vikings choose in the fifth round out of Florida State in 1986? He started the first six games in place of the injured Anthony Carter that season and showed his value with back-to-back 100-yard performances in games three and four.

46. Who did the Vikings choose as their first-round pick in 1988?

47. What All-American running back out of North Carolina State did the Vikings choose in the first round in the 1979 draft?

48. Who was the last running back picked in the first round by the Vikings?

The Draft and Trades Answers

1. Tommy Mason, Tulane

2. $10,000

3. Rip Hawkins, of North Carolina

4. Francis Asbury Tarkenton

5. Paul Dickson

6. Mick Tingelhoff

7. Karl Kassulke

8. Joe Kapp

The Draft and Trades—Answers

9. Bobby Bryant

10. Clint Jones and Gene Washington

11. Michigan State

12. Alan Page

13. Tommy Mason

14. Fran Tarkenton. Part of the New York Giants trade was their 1967 first-round pick going to the Vikings.

15. The Vikings had the first pick, and they chose Ron Yary.

16. First round

17. Jim Marshall

18. Wally Hilgenberg

19. Vince Lombardi

20. Quarterback Gary Cuozzo

21. Leo Hayden

22. 1969

23. Bobby Moore, who later took the name Ahmad Rashad

The Draft and Trades—Answers

24. Chris Doleman

25. Jim Dunaway, out of Mississippi State, but they failed to sign him (in 1963)

26. Carl Eller

27. 1964

28. The University of Minnesota

29. Fred McNeill, who they converted to outside linebacker

30. Willie Teal

31. Doug Martin

32. Tommy Kramer in 1977

33. Tackle Tim Irwin

34. USC

35. Keith Millard, from Washington State

36. 10

37. Jesse Solomon

38. The New England Patriots

The Draft and Trades—Answers

39. 1988

40. Rufus Bess, who signed originally with the Raiders as a free agent in 1979

41. Gary Zimmerman

42. 1982

43. Marcus Allen (the Heisman winner), Gerald Riggs, and Joe Morris

44. Carl Lee

45. Hassan Jones

46. Offensive guard Randall McDaniel, Arizona State

47. Ted Brown

48. D.J. Dozier, Penn State, in 1987

Photographs—Questions

1. Can you name this player (58)? He was the Vikings' first middle linebacker.

Photographs—Questions

2. Who is this slashing running back from the Vikings' early days?

Photographs—Questions

3. Do you recognize this bruising Vikings running back?

Photographs—Questions

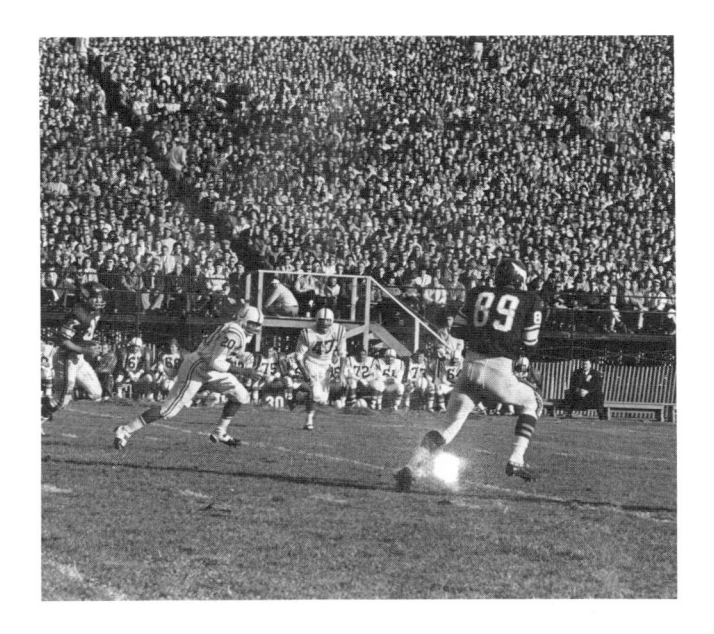

4. Who is this Vikings' tight end (89)? He was the first Minnesota end to be selected to the Pro Bowl.

Photographs—Questions

5. Name this Hall of Fame running back who anchored the Vikings ground game in 1961-62.

Photographs—Questions

6. Can you identify this quarterback who led the Vikings to Super Bowl IV?

80

Photographs—Questions

7. What were these Vikings cheerleaders called?

Photographs—Questions

8. Old Number 70 played 19 years for the Vikings. Who is this defensive end?

Photographs—Questions

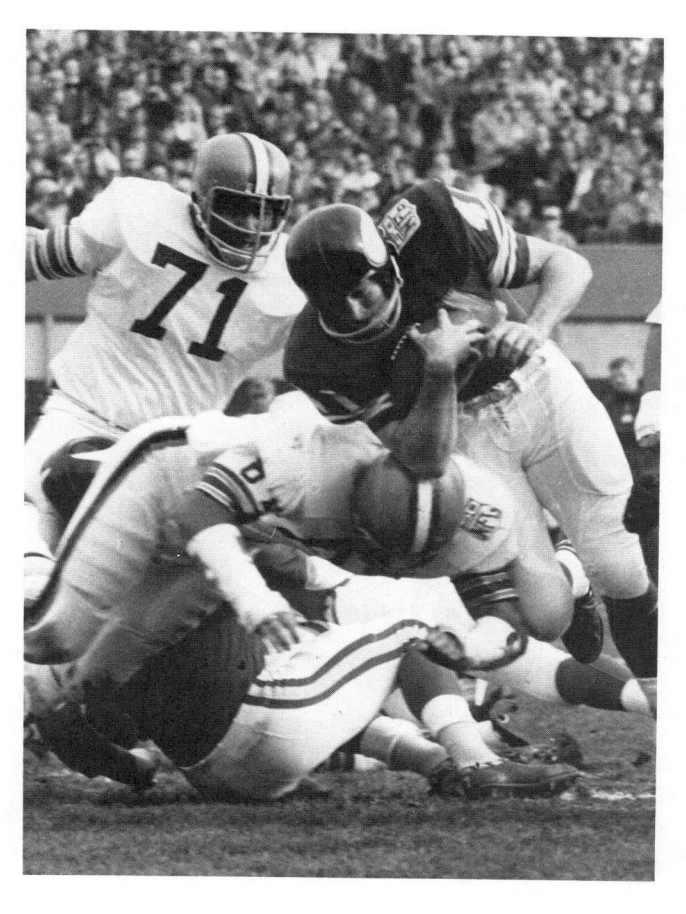

9. This player led the Vikings in rushing and receiving yardage in 1967. Who is he?

83

Photographs—Questions

10. Can you name this defensive tackle (76) who played from 1961 through 1970?

Photographs—Questions

11. This player kicked for the Vikings from 1963 through 1977 and established nearly all the team (and several NFL) kicking and scoring records.

Photographs—Questions

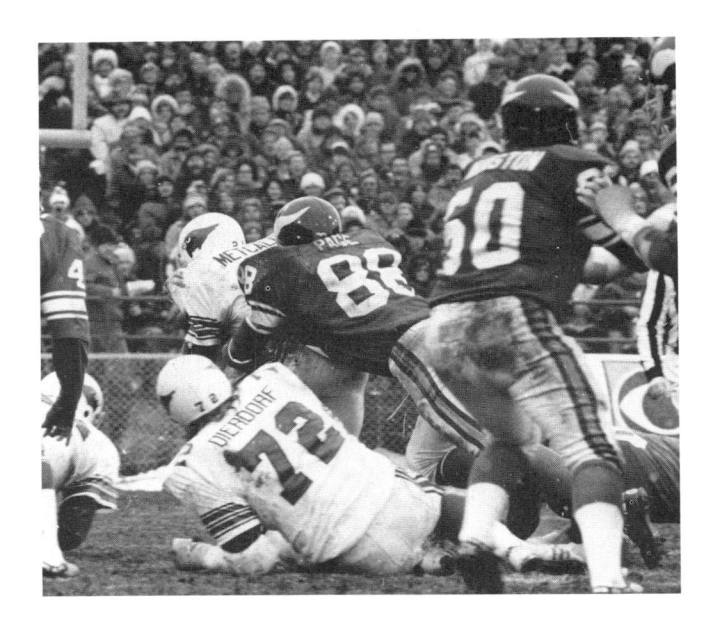

12. When was Alan Page (88) inducted in the NFL Hall Of Fame?

Photographs—Questions

13. Who is this Vikings wide receiver? He was selected to the Pro Bowl in all four years he played for the Vikings and in 1973 he made All-Pro.

87

Photographs—Questions

14. In his great career with the Vikings and Giants, Fran Tarkenton was picked for the Pro Bowl nine times. How many years did he win this honor as a Viking?

Photographs—Questions

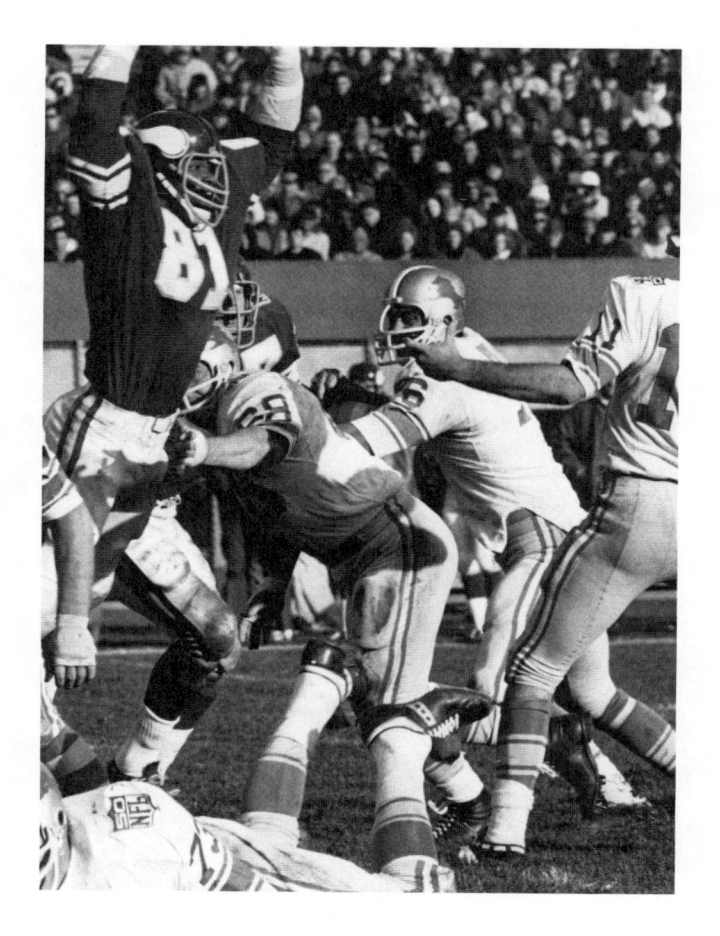

15. How many times was Carl Eller (81) selected for the Pro Bowl?

89

Photographs—Questions

16. This running back's combined rushing/receiving yardage in 1981 was only four yards shy of the single-season Vikings record. Who is he?

Photographs—Questions

17. The Vikings chose this great wide receiver in the second round of the 1976 draft. What is his name?

Photographs—Questions

18. What is head coach Bud Grant's full name?

Photographs—Questions

19. In what year did this Vikings quarterback pass for his career high of 3,912 yards?

Photographs—Questions

20. This running back holds many Vikings rushing records. Who is he?

Photographs—Questions

21. This quarterback led the Vikings to within a game of Super Bowl XXII. Can you name him?

Photographs—Questions

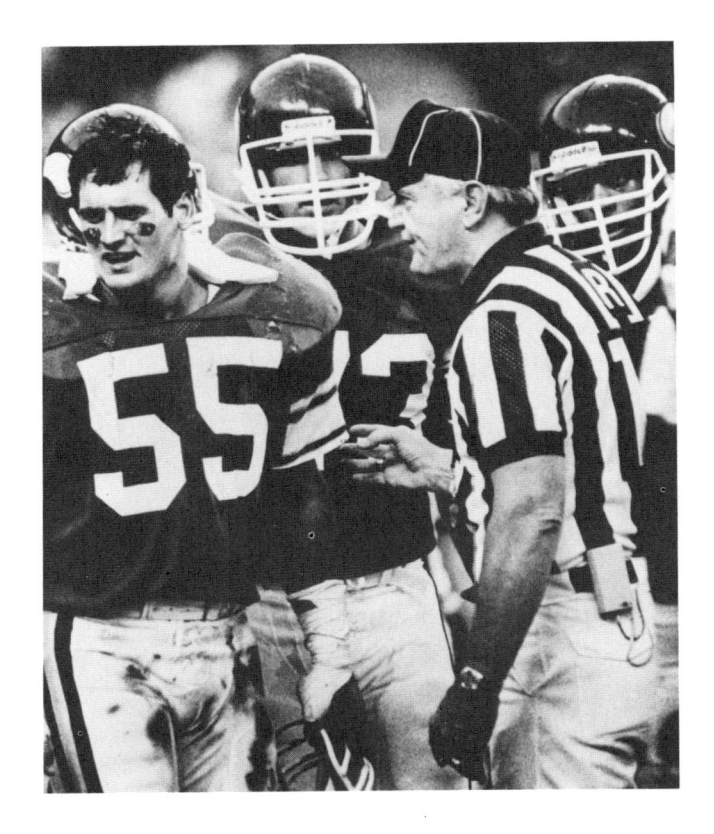

22. Can you name this Vikings defensive leader (55)?

Photographs—Questions

23. Who is this high-flying back? The Vikings chose him in the first round of the 1987 draft.

Photographs—Questions

24. What was Jerry Burns's record in his first two seasons as Vikings head coach?

Photographs
Answers

1. Rip Hawkins

2. Tommy Mason

3. Bill Brown

4. Jerry Reichow

5. Hugh McElhenny

6. Joe Kapp

7. The Parketts, from St. Louis Park (Minnesota) High School

Photographs—Answers

8. Jim Marshall

9. Dave Osborn

10. Paul Dickson

11. Fred Cox

12. July, 1988

13. John Gilliam

14. He was selected five times while playing for Minnesota.

15. Six Times

16. Ted Brown

17. Sammy White

18. Harry Peter Grant, Junior

19. Tommy Kramer's greatest passing-yardage season was in 1981.

20. Chuck Foreman

21. Wade Wilson

Photographs—Answers

22. Scott Studwell

23. D.J. Dozier

24. 17 wins and 14 losses in regular-season play and 2 wins and 1 loss in the playoffs

Miscellaneous Questions

1. Who was the first player in NFL history to play out his option and become free to join another team?

2. What major league sports team was in Minnesota before the Vikings?

3. The NFL required the Vikings to sell 25,000 season tickets before their first year of play could begin. What was the name of the civic group that took on the bulk of this project and succeeded in satisfying the NFL's demand?

Miscellaneous—Questions

4. How many NFL veteran players were sent to stock the expansion Vikings by the other NFL teams?

5. By 1967, only one of these original players remained on the Vikings. Who was he?

6. Who was the "Dutchman"?

7. What are the Vikings' official team colors?

8. When was the Vikings' first season?

9. Ticket sales for the Vikings' first season were hindered by the emergence of what local football team to national attention?

10. Who was the first person hired by the Vikings' owners? He was hired as head scout.

11. Where was the Vikings' first training camp held?

12. After a lackluster preseason who did Norm Van Brocklin and his Vikings play in their first regular-season game?

13. Rookie Fran Tarkenton had a brilliant opening-day performance. What was his completion percentage?

Miscellaneous—Questions

14. How many touchdown passes did he throw that afternoon?

15. What was the final score of the Vikings' first game?

16. What Hall of Fame defensive lineman said the following about his first experience with Fran Tarkenton and Fran's new invention, the scrambling quarterback? "We were going up against this young kid and I thought it would be easy. Then he started running around back there. I had him one time, I thought...so I really cut loose, and what happens? He's going the other way and I'm tackling air. It was like he had eyes in the back of his head...unless he heard me huffing and puffing behind him."

17. Who was the Vikings' MVP in 1970?

18. Why did Bud Grant refuse to allow warming devices on the Vikings' sideline no matter what the weather?

19. What number did Mick Tingelhoff wear?

20. What Hall of Fame running back served as the color commentator on Vikings radio, KSTP, in 1970?

Miscellaneous—Questions

21. What quarterback has the Vikings' best career passing percentage?

22. Who has the Vikings' third-best career passing percentage?

23. Which former Viking holds the all-time NFL record for the most seasons with one club?

24. What was Bud Grant referring to when he said, "There's no point in waiting until we're out there and they start playing, to decide how we're going to do it. We'll do it the right way and the same way every Sunday."

25. Of the 24 Vikings regulars in 1971, how many were from Big Ten schools?

26. Can you name those players?

27. Over the years, the Vikings' basketball team has played hundreds of games with local teams throughout the Vikings' region. Which two players started this team that has been so successful in spreading good will and helping worthy causes?

28. In what year were more Vikings players chosen for the Pro Bowl than any other?

Miscellaneous—Questions

29. How many Vikings players were selected for that year's game?

30. Name the Minnesota players who were chosen.

31. What Vikings player has scored more points than the next three highest scoring Minnesota players combined?

32. How many points did he score?

    a) 480
    b) 639
    c) 1,174
    d) 1,365

33. Who are the Vikings' next three leading scorers?

34. In the late 1960s and early 1970s, how many consecutive victories did the Vikings have over the Detroit Lions?

35. Who was selected the NFL's most valuable player in 1975?

36. In what year did the Vikings move indoors to the Hubert Humphrey Metrodome?

Miscellaneous—Questions

37. What is the football seating capacity of the Metrodome?

    a) 52,312
    b) 62,345
    c) 64,824
    d) 67,102

38. What year did Joe Kapp win the Vikings' MVP award?

39. Who holds NFL's all-time consecutive game scoring record?

40. He put points on the scoreboard in how many games in a row?

41. Where did Chuck Foreman play his college ball?

42. Who were the Vikings' offensive and defensive captains in 1977?

43. Who was the Vikings' MVP in 1967?

44. What Vikings running back out of Illinois was a Big Ten shot-put champion?

45. What is the nickname of the NLF's Central Division?

46. Who leads the NFL in career passing attempts with 6,467?

Miscellaneous—Questions

47. What player was the lone Viking chosen for the Pro Bowl in 1984?

48. Who were the three Vikings selected for the Pro Bowl in 1986?

49. The smallest home crowd in Vikings history was 13,911 at the Metrodome on October 4, 1987. Who were the Vikings playing?

50. The largest Vikings home crowd was on October 19, 1986 at the Metrodome. How many were in attendance that day against the Chicago Bears?

51. Who has passed for more yards than any other player in the history of the NFL?

52. How many times was Vikings tackle Ron Yary named to the all-pro team?

53. From 1983 through 1986 No Vikings player was selected all-pro. Who were the two Vikings that won this honor in 1987?

54. Name the six Vikings players selected for the 1987 Pro Bowl.

55. Who holds the Vikings' record for the most all-pro selections?

Miscellaneous—Questions

56. What uniform numbers, if any, have been retired by the Vikings?

57. What Vikings wide receiver's father played with Bud Grant in the Canadian Football League, eventually becoming a member of the CFL Hall of Fame? He passed on his name to his son.

58. From 1961 through 1987 how many players have played quarterback for the Vikings?

59. What is the Vikings' opening-day record through 1987?

60. What weight was offensive guard/tackle Curtis Rouse listed at in 1987?

61. What relation is former Vikings kick returner Eddie Payton to former Chicago Bears running back Walter Payton?

62. What foreign city was chosen as the site for the August 24, 1988 exhibition game between the Vikings and Bears?

Miscellaneous Answers

1. Bud Grant

2. The Minneapolis Lakers of the National Basketball Association

3. The Minneapolis Minutemen

4. 36

5. Grady Alderman

6. Norm Van Brocklin

7. Purple and white with gold trim

Miscellaneous—Answers

8. 1961

9. The Minnesota Gophers, who won the national collegiate championship in 1960.

10. Joe Thomas

11. Bemidji, Minnesota

12. The Chicago Bears

13. 74%; he completed 17 of 23 passes.

14. Four

15. Vikings 37, Bears 13

16. Gino Marchetti of the Baltimore Colts

17. Fred Cox

18. Because he read about a military study on Eskimos that said their ability to withstand cold better than military personnel was mental, not physical.

19. 53

20. Paul Hornung

21. Fran Tarkenton at 57.6%

Miscellaneous—Answers

22. Archie Manning, 55.3 percent in 1983-84

23. Jim Marshall, 19

24. He was discussing standing at attention for the National Anthem. This style of lining up became known as "The Grant Formation."

25. Eight

26. Milt Sunde, Carl Eller, Paul Krause, Wally Hilgenberg, Jim Marshall, Gene Washington, Clint Jones, John Henderson

27. Karl Kassulke and Earsell Mackbee

28. 1975

29. Nine

30. Bobby Bryant, Chuck Foreman, John Gilliam, Paul Krause, Alan Page, Jeff Siemon, Fran Tarkenton, Ed White, Ron Yary

31. Fred Cox

32. d) 1,365 points

33. Bill Brown, Chuck Foreman, Rick Danmeier

Miscellaneous—Answers

34. 13, from October, 1968 to October, 1974

35. Fran Tarkenton

36. 1982

37. b) 62,345

38. 1969

39. Fred Cox

40. 151, 1963-1973

41. The University of Miami

42. Offense, Mick Tingelhoff; defense, Jim Marshall

43. Dave Osborn

44. Bill Brown

45. "The Black and Blue Division," because of the rough play of teams such as the Vikings, Bears, Lions, and Packers

46. Fran Tarkenton

47. Kicker Jan Stenerud

48. Tommy Kramer, quarterback; Joey Browner, safety; Steve Jordan, tight end

Miscellaneous—Answers

49. The Green Bay Packers. Most of the regular players were on strike and replacement players were used by both teams.

50. 62,851

51. Fran Tarkenton, 47,003, 1961-1978

52. Five times, 1971, 1973-76

53. Safety Joey Browner and offensive tackle Gary Zimmerman

54. Joey Browner, safety; Anthony Carter, wide receiver; Chris Doleman, defensive end; Steve Jordan, tight end; Scott Studwell, linebacker; Gary Zimmerman, offensive tackle

55. Mick Tingelhoff

56. Number 10, in honor of Fran Tarkenton

57. Leo Lewis, Senior. His son, of course, is Leo Lewis, Jr.

58. 16

59. 16-10-1

60. 335 pounds

61. Eddie is Walter Payton's older brother.

62. Goteborg, Sweden

Team Records Questions

1. How many games did the Vikings win in their first season?

2. In what year did the Vikings force the opposition to punt for a team-record 99 times?

3. When did the Vikings have their first winning season?

4. On December 13, 1964, the Vikings trailed the Chicago Bears by a score of 14-0. But they came back to set a team record (since broken) for margin of victory. How many points did the Vikings win by that afternoon against the Bears?

Team Records—Questions

5. One of the Vikings' few wins in 1967 was over the division champions on the road. What was the great team the Vikings beat in a hard fought 10-7 game that year?

6. The Vikings lost to the division champs at home later that year. What was the score?

7. In 1967, the Vikings played another strong team to a 20-20 tie. Which team was that?

8. What year did the Vikings begin Central Division play? They were 3-8-3 that year behind Green Bay, Chicago, and Detroit.

9. The Vikings' defense set a team record for lowest pass completion percentage defense in 1967. What was the completion percentage of opposition passers that year?

10. There were two seasons in which the Vikings lost 11 games. When were these seasons?

11. After beating Atlanta in the first game of 1968, the Vikings played Green Bay. What happened?

12. In what year did the Vikings give up the most net yards, 6,352 in all?

Team Records—Questions

13. What year did the Vikings win their first NFC Central Division Championship?

14. What place in the Central Division did the Vikings finish the previous year?

15. In what year did the Vikings rush for a team high 20 touchdowns?

16. How many games in a row did the Vikings win in 1969? It is the longest consecutive win streak in team history.

17. In 1969 and 1977 the Vikings gave up their fewest number of field goals. How many field goals did their opponents make in each of those two record-setting years?

18. Against the Cowboys on October 18, 1970, the Vikings scored their highest single-game, regular-season point total. How many points did they score?

19. The highest number of penalty yards against the Vikings was 1,075. In what year was this total assessed against them?

20. In 1971, the Vikings' defense held its opponents to the fewest number of rushing touchdowns in team history, tying the 1934 Lions and the 1968 Cowboys for the all-time NFL record. How many rushing touchdowns did the 1971 Vikings allow?

Team Records—Questions

21. In what years were the Vikings undefeated in preseason play?

22. The fewest passing yards made against the Vikings in a single season was 1,442. In what year was the Viking opposition held to this passing yardage?

23. In 1975, how many successive games did the Vikings win at the start of the season?

24. What was the team's regular-season record that year?

25. After their Super Bowl IV loss to Kansas City, the Vikings opened the next season by playing the Super Bowl champs. What was the outcome of this rematch?

26. The night before this rematch what did Bud Grant do to motivate his players?

27. The Vikings were noted for winning on the frozen turf of Metropolitan Stadium. Between 1969 and 1980, they played 23 games there on or after December 10. What was their record in these winter games?

28. The fewest passing and rushing attempts by a Vikings' team occurred in what year?

Team Records—Questions

29. What event made this year so low in passing and rushing attempts?

30. The fewest losses by the Vikings in a single regular season was two by five different teams. Name these five record-setting years in which the Vikings lost only twice during the regular season.

31. The Vikings intercepted a team-high 30 passes in what year?

32. The most field goals made against the Vikings in a single season was 29. In what year did Viking opponents set this record?

33. In what season did the Vikings gain their most net yards?

34. The greatest number of rushing attempts by the Vikings, 556, were made in what year?

35. The fewest rushing yards allowed by the Vikings in a game came against San Francisco on December 14, 1969. How many rushing yards did the 49ers gain that day?

36. On November 20, 1970, the pre-Payton Chicago Bears rushed for more yards against the Vikings than any other team in Vikings' history. How many yards did the Bears rush for that afternoon?

Team Records—Questions

37. What is the Vikings' team defensive record for the most passes intercepted in a single game?

38. How many net passing yards did the Vikings defense limit New Orleas to on November 16, 1975, to establish the team single-game record?

39. On consecutive Sundays in November, 1975, against Atlanta and New Orleans, the Vikings' defense held their opposition to the same number of net yards. It was the fewest single-game net yards ever allowed by Minnesota. How many yards did the Vikings allow?

40. The most rushing yardage attained by the Vikings occurred in what year?

41. In what season did the Vikings attempt the most passes?

42. How many passes did they attempt that year?

43. The fewest pass attempts by the Vikings in a season has been 282. What was the year?

44. The fewest first downs by a Vikings team in a single game came against Green Bay on November 14, 1971. How many first downs did the Vikings make that day?

Team Records—Questions

45. In 1978, the Vikings had more of their passes intercepted than in any other year. How many were intercepted?

46. In 1980, the Vikings gave up their fewest number of fumbles. How many fumbles did the opposition recover that year?

47. The fewest net yards allowed by the Vikings in a season was in what year?

48. In 1975 and 1986, the Vikings scored their highest number of touchdowns. How many touchdowns did they score in each of those seasons?

49. What team have the Vikings defeated more times than any other?

50. What is the Vikings' record in the 53 games the two teams have played?

51. Only once have the Vikings held an opponent to no first downs rushing in a single game. It happened at Metropolitan Stadium against San Francisco on December 14 of what year?

52. What was the Vikings' 1986 preseason record?

53. What are the most games ever won by a Vikings' team during the regular season?

Team Records—Questions

54. What are the fewest number of games won by the Vikings during the regular season?

55. Behind quarterback Joe Kapp the Vikings amassed their greatest single-day total offense in a game against Baltimore on September 28, 1969. How many total net yards did the Vikings accumulate that afternoon?

56. How many of the total yards in the game against Baltimore were passing yards?

57. The Vikings' defense set the team record for sacks against Chicago on November 2, 1969, and tied it against Atlanta on December 20, 1970. How many sacks did the defense have on each of those record-setting days?

58. In a 1967 game, the Vikings' defense forced 11 fumbles, still the team record. Who was the hapless opponent?

59. The most penalties and greatest penalty yardage ever levied against a Vikings' opponent in one game was 16 penalties for 140 yards on October 14, 1984. What team was penalized so heavily?

60. In beating the Vikings on October 6, 1963, St. Louis scored the highest number of points ever against the Vikings. How many points did St. Louis score?

Team Records—Questions

61. Chicago sacked the Vikings' quarterback a record number of times on October 28, 1984. How many sacks did the Bears record?

62. The Vikings' greatest margin of loss came on December 8, 1984. Who were the Vikings playing that day when they were defeated by 44 points?

63. After the return of Bud Grant in 1985, the Vikings opened their season with the defending Super Bowl-champion San Francisco 49ers at the Metrodome. What was the outcome of that game?

64. The greatest margin of victory by the Vikings in a single game was over Cleveland on November 9, 1969. What was the point difference?

65. The fewest points scored by the Vikings in a win was against Green Bay on November 14, 1971. How many points did they score that day?

66. In what year did the Vikings give up the fewest points to their opposition in the regular season?

67. How many points did the Vikings' defense give up to opposing teams that year?

Team Records—Questions

68. What are the most interceptions the Vikings have thrown in a single game? It has happened several times, most recently against the Bears (October 27, 1985).

69. Against Green Bay on November 11, 1971, the Vikings had their fewest net yards in a single game. How many net yards did their offense make that day?

70. What was the Vikings' season record in 1985 when Bud Grant coached his final year?

71. Under rookie coach Jerry Burns what record did the Vikings compile in 1986?

72. Led by running backs Bill Brown and Tommy Mason, the Vikings rushed for a team single-game yardage record against Baltimore on September 13, 1964. How many yards did the Vikings gain?

73. The Vikings' team record for least number of passing touchdowns allowed in a season is six. When was this record set?

74. The record for the most passing touchdowns allowed by a Vikings' team was set in 1984. How many passing touchdowns did opponents score that year?

Team Records—Questions

75. While compiling a 9-7 record in regular season play, the 1986 Vikings led the NFC in what team offensive category?

76. In what three consecutive years did the Vikings' defense lead the NFL in fewest points allowed?

77. Through 1987, the Vikings have scored first in 187 regular season games. How many of these did the Vikings go on to win?

78. Through 1987, what is the regular-season winning percentage of the Vikings?

Team Records Answers

1. Three

2. 1969

3. 1964, when they were 8-5

4. 37 points, as they beat the Bears 41-14

5. The Green Bay Packers, who went on to win Super Bowl II.

6. The Packers won 30-27

7. The Baltimore Colts

8. 1967

Team Records—Answers

9. 47.4 percent

10. 1961 and 1962

11. The Vikings defeated the Super Bowl-champion Packers 26-13.

12. 1984

13. 1968

14. Fourth

15. 1987

16. 12; they lost only their first and last games of the regular season.

17. Only seven each year

18. 54, winning 54-13 over Dallas

19. 1967

20. Two

21. 1964, 1965, and 1973, going 5-0 in each preseason

22. 1970

23. 10

Team Records—Answers

24. 12–2

25. The Vikings defeated the Chiefs 27-10.

26. He showed them the Super Bowl highlights film.

27. 19-4

28. 1982

29. The players strike which shortened the regular season from 16 weeks to 9

30. 1969, 1970, 1973, 1975 and 1976

31. 1969

32. 1985

33. 1981, 5,845

34. 1975

35. The Vikings' defense held San Francisco to 12 yards rushing.

36. 343 yards

37. 5, several times

38. A minus 7 yards

39. Only 60 net yards in each game

Team Records—Answers

40. 1965, 2,279

41. 1981

42. 709

43. 1968

44. Five

45. 34

46. Three

47. 1969, only 2,720

48. 48

49. Detroit

50. 33 wins, 18 losses, and 2 ties

51. 1969, and the Vikings won 10-7

52. 3 wins and 1 loss. They beat Miami, Denver, and Indianapolis and lost to Seattle.

53. 12, in 1969, 1970, 1973 and 1975

54. Two, in 1962

Team Records—Answers

55. 622 yards

56. 530 yards

57. The defense had nine sacks in each game.

58. The Detroit Lions

59. The Los Angeles Raiders

60. 56 points in winning 56-14

61. 11

62. San Francisco, 51-7

63. The Vikings beat the 49ers 28-2.

64. 48 points (51-3)

65. 3 in a 3-0 win

66. 1969

67. 133 points

68. Five

69. 87 yards

70. 7 wins, 9 losses

71. 9 wins, 7 losses for second place in the NFC Central Division

Team Records—Answers

72. 313 yards

73. 1970

74. 35

75. Points scored with 398, which is also the club record

76. 1969-71

77. 136, for a .720 winning percentage

78. .542, 207-174-9

Postseason Questions

1. Who did the Vikings play in their first division playoff game on December 22, 1968?

2. Joe Kapp had a big passing day for the Vikings, throwing for 287 yards. How many touchdown passes did he have?

3. How many passes did running back Bill Brown catch?

4. Despite Kapp's performance, what was the final score?

5. In what year did the Vikings win their first playoff game?

Postseason—Questions

6. Who did they beat in that first playoff victory?

7. What was the score at halftime?

8. The Rams were in the same man-to-man defense they employed in their regular-season loss to the Vikings when they held the top Vikings receiver to no receptions. What receiver took advantage of the Rams' single coverage this time, catching four passes for 90 yards, including a 41-yard strike that set up the second Minnesota touchdown?

9. The touchdown that put the Vikings ahead for good came on a play where halfback Dave Osborn and guard Jim Vellone blocked for a run to the outside. Who carried the ball on this play designed to be used when the middle of the defensive line gets tough near the goal line?

10. How were the last Vikings' points put on the board?

11. With less than a minute to go, a Vikings' defensive lineman intercepted a Roman Gabriel pass and returned it 29 yards to the Rams' 26 where the Vikings let the time run out. Who sealed the victory and the Vikings' first conference championship with this last minute interception?

Postseason—Questions

12. What was the final score?

13. What team did the Vikings beat in their next playoff game for the NFL championship?

14. Against Cleveland, the Vikings scored on their first two possessions. Who made the first touchdown?

15. On the second score, Kapp threw the longest Vikings postseason touchdown pass. Who was the receiver who caught this 75-yard touchdown strike?

16. Who led the Vikings in rushing with 108 yards?

17. Which Vikings running back took the ball in from the Cleveland 20-yard line for the Vikings' third touchdown?

18. On what date did the Vikings play their first Super Bowl?

19. How many points were the Vikings favored over the Kansas City Chiefs in Super Bowl IV?

20. In Super Bowl IV, what Vikings player dislocated his shoulder with eight minutes remaining?

Postseason—Questions

21. Who scored the Vikings' only touchdown in Super Bowl IV?

22. What player had the highest number of receiving yards in Super Bowl IV?

23. After Super Bowl IV, what defensive back said, "We made more mistakes today than we did in 22 games."

24. How many turnovers did the Vikings have in Super Bowl IV compared with the Chiefs?

25. What was the final score in Super Bowl IV?

26. Who was the MVP in Super Bowl IV?

27. What Viking postseason rushing record did Dave Osborn set in 1969?

28. In 1970, the Vikings made the playoffs but were defeated in the opening game. Who beat them on December 27, 1970 at Metropolitan Stadium by a score of 17-14?

29. The lack of a proven quarterback contributed to a 20-12 Vikings' playoff loss to what team in 1971?

Postseason—Questions

30. What was the Vikings' record in 1972 after the return of Fran Tarkenton from the New York Giants? It was the first season in five years the team failed to make the playoffs.

31. On December 22, 1973, the Vikings won the divisional playoff game at Metropolitan Stadium by a score of 27-20. What team did they defeat?

32. With the Vikings trailing by four points at halftime, a player brought the locker room to attention by smashing a blackboard to pieces and then in a booming voice delivered this speech: "We've gone too damn far to play like this. We are so tight out there we're embarrassing ourselves. Let's relax and play our game." Who was he?

33. After this fiery outburst, how many of their 27 points did the Vikings score in the second half?

34. The Vikings capitalized on a Redskins' defensive back who had replaced injured regular Ted Vactor. Who was this Washington substitute who had not played cornerback in four years? He was noted for his breakaway kickoff returns.

35. Name the Vikings receiver who beat him for two touchdowns.

Postseason—Questions

36. A successful Vikings running game complemented their passing attack against the Redskins. Who was the leading Minnesota ground gainer with 95 yards on 17 carries?

37. This was the Vikings' first playoff victory since what season?

38. What team did the Vikings play in the NFC Championship Game on December 30, 1973?

39. According to Dallas coach Tom Landry, the "key play" happened in the third quarter. "We were only down 10-7, the crowd was catching fire, then the long pass took everything away...that was the most critical play." Which Vikings receiver caught the "rainbow pass," as Bud Grant called it, a touchdown that turned the game around?

40. How much distance did the pass cover?

41. The Vikings made major changes in their offense to confuse the disciplined, highly regimented defense of the Cowboys, adding such plays as the "double sucker," "YMCA," and counter-step. Which Vikings coach came up with these plays that proved so effective?

Postseason—Questions

42. Which Minnesota defensive back intercepted a pass and returned it a Vikings' postseason record 63 yards for the final touchdown?

43. What did the final score turn out to be at the end of this NFC Championship Game?

44. Who did the Vikings play in Super Bowl VIII, their second Super Bowl?

45. What was the date of Super Bowl VIII?

46. Where was Super Bowl VIII played?

47. Going into the game what Vikings player had the best rushing average per carry?

48. The Dolphins' running attack was built on the strength of their fullback and the lightning speed of their halfback. Who were these two great running backs?

49. Of the two, which one did the most damage to the Vikings that afternoon by rushing for 145 yards?

50. The Dolphins had a defense that held opponents to 176 points in 16 games; one of its key aspects was substituting a linebacker for a defensive tackle. What was the name of this special defense?

Postseason—Questions

51. Who was the Vikings' leading rusher in Super Bowl VIII?

52. Who was the Vikings' head coach in Super Bowl VIII and also in their other three Super Bowl appearances?

53. Who was the head coach for the Dolphins in Super Bowl VIII?

54. Trailing 17-0 just before the end of the first half, the Vikings chose to run instead of kicking a field goal on fourth and one from the Dolphins' 6. What happened?

55. To start the second half, John Gilliam ran the kickoff back 65 yards to the Dolphins' 34-yard line. What nullified his return?

56. How many pass attempts did Bob Griese and the Dolphins try against the Vikings?

57. How many rushing attempts did the Vikings' rookie of the year, Chuck Foreman, have against the Dolphins?

58. How many net yards rushing did the Vikings gain?

59. What was the final score in Super Bowl VIII?

Postseason—Questions

60. Who scored the Vikings' only touchdown?

61. Who was the MVP in Super Bowl VIII?

62. What was the Vikings' regular-season record in 1974?

63. Who did the Vikings play on December 21, 1974 at Metropolitan Stadium in the NFC Divisional Playoff Game?

64. After a sluggish first half on the part of both teams the score was tied at 7-7. Two "Christmas Presents," as Bud Grant later called them, shifted the game in the Vikings' favor. What was the first "Christmas Present"? It occurred on the third play of the second half.

65. Two plays after the Cox field goal, the second "Christmas Present" was handed to the Vikings. What happened on this play to put Minnesota up by 10 points in a matter of seconds?

66. Who was the Vikings' cornerback who took advantage of these two "Christmas presents"?

67. Four minutes later, a Vikings receiver put the game out of the Cardinals reach with a 38-yard touchdown reception from Fran Tarkenton. It was his second touchdown catch of the day. Who was this wide receiver?

Postseason—Questions

68. What was the final score in this one-sided Vikings' victory?

69. What team did the Vikings play the next week at Metropolitan Stadium for the NFC championship?

70. In the game the Rams forced the Vikings to run up the middle by shutting down their outside running attack and by keeping Fran Tarkenton boxed up and unable to do much scrambling. How many running plays did the Vikings attempt in gaining 164 tough yards on the ground that day?

71. Despite Minnesota's emphasis on the running game, the first score came through the air on a 29-yard pass. Who scored the Vikings' first touchdown?

72. The big defensive play of the game came with six minutes left in the third quarter and the Vikes up by only 10-3. The Rams had marched 98 yards to the Vikings' half-yard line. As the teams were getting ready to come off the ball, a Viking lineman allegedly saw a slight movement in the Rams' offensive line; he jumped offside and made contact hoping to draw a penalty on the Rams. The gamble worked and the ball was taken back to the five. Which Viking took this chance and backed Los Angeles away from the goal line?

Postseason—Questions

73. Two plays later, a Vikings' linebacker intercepted a James Harris pass in the end zone. Who made this touchback?

74. After the interception, the Vikings drove down the field from their own 20 to the Rams 1-yard line. What running back scored the winning touchdown on a plunge over the middle?

75. What was the final score at the end of this "toe to toe" NFC Championship Game?

76. Who did the Vikings play in Super Bowl IX on January 12, 1975?

77. Who was the Steelers' owner?

78. The Steelers had gone over forty years without winning a championship of any kind until they finished in first place in their division in what year?

79. Who was the Steelers' head coach?

80. What Steelers defensive lineman picked up his nickname a few years earlier in a game against the Giants because of a late tackle on then Giants quarterback Fran Tarkenton?

81. What team was favored to win Super Bowl IX?

Postseason—Questions

82. What was the score at the end of the first half?

83. Which Viking fumbled the third quarter kickoff setting up a Pittsburgh touchdown?

84. How many of Fran Tarkenton's passes were intercepted?

85. What Viking recovered a blocked punt in the end zone for a touchdown?

86. How many offensive touchdowns did the Vikings score in Super Bowls VIII and IX combined?

87. The Steelers set a Super Bowl record for rushing attempts in Super Bowl IX. How many running plays did they make to set the record?

88. Who was the MVP in Super Bowl IX?

89. Steeler equipment manager Tony Parisi is credited with giving Pittsburgh a major advantage in the game. What did he do that may have turned the tide in favor of the Steelers?

90. Chuck Foreman led all receivers in the game. How many yards did he make receiving?

Postseason—Questions

91. How many net rushing yards did the Steelers' defense hold the Vikings to in Super Bowl IX?

92. Which player set the Vikings' single-game postseason solo tackle record in Super Bowl IX?

93. What was the final score in Super Bowl IX?

94. In qualifying for the divisional playoffs in 1975, what regular-season record did the Vikings have that year?

95. Who did the Vikings lose to by a score of 17-14 at Metropolitan Stadium in the 1975 divisional playoff game?

96. In the game, which Vikings defensive lineman sacked the Cowboys' Roger Staubach a postseason record three times.

97. The infamous "Hail Mary" pass turned the game in the Cowboys' favor when, with 32 seconds to go, Roger Staubach threw a 50-yard pass that went for a touchdown. Who caught the ball for Dallas?

Postseason—Questions

98. The Vikings contested the play because of what appeared to be offensive pass interference when Pearson made contact with a Minnesota defender just in front of the end zone. Who was the Vikings' defensive back who did not get the call from the officials?

99. This game also marked the end to allowing glass containers in the stands at Metropolitan Stadium. What did the normally stoic Minnesota fans do after this play?

100. The Vikings again qualified for the playoffs in 1976 by posting an 11-2-1 record. Who was their opponent in the divisional playoff game at Metropolitan Stadium on December 18, 1976?

101. On the fourth play of the game the Vikings scored on an 18-yard pass. Name the Vikings receiver who, after being hit on the 10 by a Redskins linebacker, proceeded to carry the linebacker and several of his teammates for a ride on his back into the end zone.

102. Which Vikings receiver caught two touchdown passes: one a 27-yard pass in the first quarter and the other a nine yard completion for the final Vikings' score in the third?

Postseason—Questions

103. Two Vikings backs ran for over 100 yards each against the Redskins. One was Chuck Foreman who said about their performance, "If they key on me, I'll block for _____. If they start getting after him, he blocks for me. We're the dynamic duo." Who was the other running back in the Vikings' powerful one-two punch against the Redskins?

104. Before the game, the Redskins' head coach said this Vikings team had the best offensive unit of any Minnesota he had ever seen. Who was the coach that made this astute observation?

105. What was the score at the end of the third quarter and at the final whistle?

106. What Vikings' postseason single-game passing record did Fran Tarkenton set in the victory over Washington?

107. The 1976 NFC Championship Game was also played at Metropolitan Stadium. What was the outcome of this game?

108. In this game a Vikings' running back ran 62 yards from scrimmage to establish a team playoff record. Who was he?

109. Who played in Super Bowl XI on January 9, 1977?

110. The Raiders advanced to the Super Bowl with a 24-7 win over what team?

Postseason—Questions

111. Where was Super Bowl XI played?

112. The game set a Super Bowl record for paid attendance. How many attended the game?

113. Who were the starting front four defensive lineman for the Vikings in Super Bowl XI?

114. Who was the former sprinter the Raiders employed as their deep threat at wide receiver?

115. What running back started next to Chuck Foreman in the Vikings' backfield?

116. On the Raiders' third possession, with no score in the game, Ray Guy (who had never had a punt blocked in his four years in the NFL) had one blocked. What Viking blocked the punt and recovered on the Raiders' 3-yard line?

117. What happened two plays later on the Raiders' 2-yard line?

118. What was the score at halftime?

119. With the Raiders leading 19-0, Fran Tarkenton threw his lone touchdown pass of the day to which Vikings receiver?

Postseason—Questions

120. How many interceptions did Tarkenton throw that day against the Raiders to go along with his one touchdown pass?

121. Who replaced Tarkenton at quarterback late in the fourth quarter, completing seven of nine passes and throwing for the Vikings' last touchdown?

122. Who caught the 13-yard pass that was the Vikings' last touchdown?

123. The Raiders connected on 12 of 19 passes under quarterback Ken Stabler's direction for 180 yards. How many passing yards did the Vikings make by completing 24 of 44 passes?

124. The Vikings gained 71 yards rushing. How many yards on the ground did the Raiders make in Super Bowl XI?

125. What was the final score in Super Bowl XI?

126. The Vikings qualified for the playoffs the next year by winning the NFC Central Division again with a 9-5 record. Who did they play on December 26, 1977, in the divisional playoff?

127. Where was the game held?

128. What team was favored to win and by how many points?

Postseason—Questions

129. What was the weather like during the game and how did it affect play?

130. Who quarterbacked the Vikings in place of the injured Fran Tarkenton?

131. Who scored first?

132. To keep the Vikings' initial drive going, Lee hit two key third-down passes. Who caught these crucial sideline throws?

133. The touchdown came on a run from five yards out. Who scored for the Vikings?

134. As the rain fell harder and the muck worsened, both offenses struggled. The score stayed 7-0 into the fourth quarter until a Vikings' reserve plunged over from the Rams' 1-yard line. Who was this running back who put the game out of reach?

135. What was the final score of this 1977 playoff game?

136. After the victory, the awarding of the game ball was handled in an unusual fashion. What happened?

137. On New Year's Day, 1978, the Vikings played in the NFC Championship Game against what team?

Postseason—Questions

138. What was the final score in that NFC Championship Game?

139. Dallas went on to face Denver in Super Bowl XII. What was the outcome of that game?

140. In 1978, the Vikings won the Central Division title with an 8-7-1 mark. Counting this 1978 title, how many years in a row had the Vikings won the Central Division?

141. In 1978, the Vikings lost the divisional playoff game to what team by a score of 34-10?

142. In what year did the Vikings win their last Central Division title?

143. What was the outcome of the Vikings January 3, 1981 divisional playoff game against Philadelphia?

144. In the strike-shortened 1982 season, who did the Vikings play at the Metrodome in the first round of the Super Bowl tournament?

145. Who led the Vikings in total catches and receiving yards against the Falcons that day by catching six balls for 81 yards?

146. Which player scored the most points in the game?

Postseason—Questions

147. What was the final score?

148. Who did the Vikings play in the second round of the 1982 Super Bowl tournament?

149. What Redskins running back gained 185 yards in 37 attempts against the Vikings' defense that afternoon in the Metrodome?

150. What was the score at halftime?

151. After the Redskins' defeat, when did the Vikings next qualify for the playoffs?

152. In 1987, who did the Vikings play in their first playoff game since the 1982 season?

153. What Vikings player caught six passes that day for 79 yards and returned six punts for 143 yards (one an NFL record-setting 84-yard punt return that went for a touchdown)?

154. How many turnovers did the Vikings force against the Saints?

155. What was the final score?

156. Who was the Vikings' next opponent?

Postseason—Questions

157. What was the halftime score?

158. Vikings quarterback Wade Wilson threw touchdown passes to which two receivers?

159. What Vikings rookie defensive back intercepted a 49ers' pass and ran it back 45 yards for a touchdown?

160. Chuck Nelson set an NFL record against San Francisco for the most field goals in a playoff game. How many did he kick?

161. Wade Wilson set a Vikings' single-game playoff record for the most passing yards. How many yards did he throw for against San Francisco?

162. Anthony Carter caught 10 passes and set an NFL playoff record for total receiving yardage in a single game. What was his total receiving yardage against San Francisco?

163. What was the final score?

164. Who did the Vikings then play for the 1987 NFC title and the right to go to the Super Bowl?

165. The score was tied at intermission. How many points did the Vikings and Redskins make in the first half?

Postseason—Questions

166. Trailing 17-10 with 56 seconds remaining in the game, the Vikings had fourth and four from the Washington six-yard line. What happened?

167. Who set a Vikings' record for punting yardage in a postseason game?

168. Who scored the Vikings' only touchdown on a 23-yard pass from Wade Wilson?

169. What offensive tackle has played in more postseason games than any Vikings player?

170. What Vikings player is second in the all-time Super Bowl records for number of career pass receptions?

171. What Vikings player has scored the most career postseason points? He has 78.

172. What Vikings player scored 36 points in a single postseason to set the team record?

173. What Vikings quarterback threw the most touchdown passes in a single postseason?

174. What two Vikings players have caught the most career postseason touchdown passes? They each have five.

Postseason—Questions

175. What Vikings player has the best career playoff rushing average?

176. With 45, which Vikings player has the most career postseason catches?

177. In the playoffs, which Viking has returned the most kickoffs? He has twice as many kickoff returns as any other Viking player.

178. Which player has the best career punting average in postseason games for the Vikings?

179. Which Vikings linebacker leads the team in career postseason blocked kicks? He has three.

180. Which Viking kicked a 46-yard field goal to establish the mark for the longest in team postseason play?

181. In what playoff game did the Vikings as a team have the most net yards?

182. In what game did the Vikings attain their greatest postseason margin of victory over an opponent?

183. The most passes intercepted in a postseason game by the Vikings' defense is four, which occurred twice, once in 1973 and again in the 1987 playoffs. What teams were the Vikings playing?

Postseason—Questions

184. What linebacker leads the Vikings in solo, assisted, and total playoff tackles?

185. What Vikings defensive back has double the playoff interceptions of any other Minnesota player?

186. What defensive lineman leads the Vikings in postseason forced fumbles with three?

187. Who has the most playoff sacks for the Vikings

Postseason Answers

1. The Baltimore Colts

2. Two

3. Eight

4. Baltimore won 24-14.

5. 1969

6. The Los Angeles Rams

7. The Vikings trailed 17-7

8. Gene Washington

Postseason—Answers

9. Quarterback Joe Kapp, who ran in from the 2-yard line

10. The last two points came on a Carl Eller safety when he tackled Roman Gabriel in the end zone.

11. Alan Page

12. Minnesota won 23-20.

13. The Vikings defeated Cleveland 27-7 in Minnesota on January 4, 1970.

14. After Bill Brown slipped on the partially frozen turf and missed the handoff Joe Kapp ran in from seven yards out.

15. Gene Washington

16. Dave Osborn

17. Dave Osborn

18. They played on January 11, 1970 in Super Bowl IV.

19. 13

20. Joe Kapp

21. Dave Osborn on a four-yard run in the third quarter

Postseason—Answers

22. Vikings wide receiver John Henderson with 111 yards

23. Karl Kassulke

24. The Vikings had five turnovers—three interceptions and two fumbles; the Chiefs recovered their only fumble and threw one interception.

25. Kansas City 23, Minnesota 7

26. Chiefs quarterback Len Dawson

27. He ran for four touchdowns in 1969 postseason play to set the record for rushing touchdowns.

28. San Francisco

29. Dallas

30. 7-7

31. The Washington Redskins

32. Carl Eller

33. 24 points, the most ever scored by the Vikings in the second half of a playoff game.

34. Speedy Duncan

Postseason—Answers

35. John Gilliam

36. Oscar Reed

37. 1969

38. The Dallas Cowboys

39. Wide receiver John Gilliam

40. 54 yards

41. Offensive coordinator Jerry Burns

42. Bobby Bryant

43. Minnesota 27, Dallas 10

44. The Miami Dolphins

45. January 13, 1974

46. Rice Stadium, Houston, Texas

47. Fran Tarkenton with 4.9 yards per carry on 41 attempts

48. Fullback Larry Csonka and halfback Mercury Morris

49. Fullback Larry Csonka

50. The "53" defense after linebacker Bob Matheson's number

Postseason—Answers

51. Oscar Reed, with 32 yards

52. Bud Grant

53. Don Shula

54. Oscar Reed fumbled and the Dolphins recovered.

55. The Vikings were called for clipping.

56. Seven, and Griese completed six for 73 yards

57. Seven attempts for 18 yards

58. 72 yards

59. Miami won 24-7.

60. Fran Tarkenton on a four-yard run

61. Larry Csonka

62. 10-4

63. The St. Louis Cardinals

64. A Vikings defensive back intercepted a Jim Hart pass when Cardinals receiver Mel Gray failed to complete his pass pattern because he was called for being offside. The Vikes declined the penalty and took the ball, scoring shortly afterward on a 37-yard field goal by Fred Cox.

Postseason—Answers

65. Cardinals running back Terry Metcalf had the ball knocked loose by Carl Eller and Alan Page when he tried to run into the left side of the Vikings' line. The same defensive back who had intercepted the Hart pass a few plays earlier picked up the ball and ran 20 yards into the St. Louis end zone.

66. Nate Wright

67. John Gilliam

68. 30-14

69. The Los Angeles Rams

70. The Vikings attempted 47 running plays for a 3.5 yard average.

71. Wide receiver Jim Lash

72. Alan Page

73. Wally Hilgenberg

74. Dave Osborn

75. The Vikings won 14-10.

76. The Pittsburgh Steelers

77. Art Rooney

Postseason—Answers

78. 1972

79. Chuck Noll

80. "Mean" Joe Greene

81. The Steelers by 3 points

82. The Steelers led 2-0 on a safety by Dwight White, who tackled Fran Tarkenton in the end zone

83. Bill Brown

84. Three

85. Terry Brown

86. One (in Super Bowl VIII)

87. 57 rushing attempts

88. Franco Harris

89. He ordered a new type of shoe for the Steelers that was ideal for playing on the slick Tulane artificial surface.

90. 50 yards on 5 catches

91. 17 net yards

92. Jeff Siemon, who had 15 solo tackles

Postseason—Answers

93. Pittsburgh 16, Minnesota 6

94. 12-2

95. Dallas, on December 28, 1975

96. Carl Eller

97. Drew Pearson

98. Nate Wright

99. They booed incessantly and one particularly irate fan, of very poor judgement, threw a whiskey bottle that struck an official.

100. The Washington Redskins

101. Tight end Stu Voigt

102. Sammy White

103. Brent McClanahan

104. George Allen

105. Minnesota led 35-6 at the end of the third quarter, and 35-20 at the end of the game.

106. He threw three touchdown passes, setting a team record for the most touchdown passes in a postseason game.

Postseason—Answers

107. The Vikings beat the Rams 24-13.

108. Chuck Foreman

109. The Vikings and the Oakland Raiders

110. The Pittsburgh Steelers, winners of the last two Super Bowls

111. At the Rose Bowl in Pasadena, California

112. 103,438

113. Carl Eller, Jim Marshall, Alan Page, and Doug Sutherland

114. Cliff Branch

115. Brent McClanahan

116. Fred McNeill

117. Brent McClanahan fumbled and the Raiders recovered.

118. Raiders 16, Vikings 0

119. Sammy White

120. He threw two interceptions, both in the second half.

121. Bobby Lee

122. Stu Voigt

Postseason—Answers

123. 282 yards

124. 266 yards

125. Oakland 32, Minnesota 14

126. The Los Angeles Rams

127. The Los Angeles Coliseum.

128. The Rams were favored by nine points.

129. A wind-driven rain fell during the game turning the field into a swamp.

130. Bobby Lee

131. The Vikings on a 70-yard drive in the first quarter

132. Ahmad Rashad

133. Chuck Foreman

134. Sammy Johnson

135. The Vikings won 14-7

136. The entire team was awarded the game ball. Forty-five inscribed footballs were given out.

137. Dallas

Postseason—Answers

138. Dallas 23, the Vikings 6

139. Dallas won 27-10.

140. Six, 1973-78

141. The Los Angeles Rams

142. 1980, with a 9-7 record

143. The Eagles won 31-16.

144. The Atlanta Falcons

145. Tight end Joe Senser

146. The Vikings' Rick Danmeier with 12 points on three field goals and three extra points

147. Vikings 30, Atlanta 24

148. The Washington Redskins

149. John Riggins

150. 21-7 Redskins, which was also the final score of the game

151. The Vikings next qualified for the playoffs by winning a wild card spot in 1987.

Postseason—Answers

152. The Vikings played the New Orleans Saints at the Superdome in New Orleans on January 3, 1988.

153. Anthony Carter

154. Six, four interceptions and two fumbles

155. Vikings 44, New Orleans 10

156. The San Francisco 49ers

157. Vikings 20, San Francisco 3

158. Tight end Carl Hilton and wide receiver Hassan Jones

159. Reggie Rutland

160. Five

161. 298 yards

162. 227 yards, he also rushed once for 30 yards and returned two punts for 21 yards for a total of 278 yards on the day

163. Vikings 36, San Francisco 24

164. The Washington Redskins

165. The score at the half was 7-7.

Postseason—Answers

166. Wade Wilson threw a pass that Darrin Nelson dropped on the goal line, and the Redskins went on to win the game. The Redskins then defeated Denver to become the 1987 Super Bowl Champions.

167. Bucky Scribner, 322 yards

168. Leo Lewis

169. Ron Yary, 21 games

170. Chuck Foreman with 15

171. Fred Cox

172. Chuck Nelson in 1987

173. Wade Wilson, who threw five touchdowns in 1987

174. Sammy White and John Gilliam

175. Joe Kapp, 5.5 yards a carry

176. Chuck Foreman

177. Charlie West, who has 20 kickoff returns

178. Bobby Lee, 40.5 yards per kick

Postseason—Answers

179. Matt Blair

180. Chuck Nelson, against San Francisco, January 9, 1988

181. Against New Orleans, January 3, 1988, the Vikings made 417 net yards.

182. They defeated New Orleans by 34 points (44-10) in the 1987 wild card game.

183. Dallas, December 20, 1973, and New Orleans, January 3, 1988

184. Wally Hilgenberg

185. Bobby Bryant, who has six interceptions

186. Alan Page

187. Carl Eller, 11; Alan Page is second with 7.5, folowed by Jim Marshall's 7

Memorable Moments Questions

Several Vikings alumni were asked what their most memorable moment was as a Vikings player in a regular or postseason game. The following questions and answers are their responses (which may have been edited slightly because of length or for clarity).

1. Which Minnesota running back's most memorable moment is the following?

   "It was in 1980 playing in the old Met Stadium against the Cleveland Browns. We were down by a point with 14 seconds left on the clock. On the first play Tommy Kramer throws to Joe

Memorable Moments—Questions

Senser, Joe pitches to me, and I run out of bounds at the 46-yard line. The next play is history, 'Hail Mary' to Ahmad Rashad, T.D.! Vikes win!!"

2. Which Vikings kicker chose the following as his most memorable moment?

"It was in the second regular-season game in 1978 at Denver on Monday Night Football. I kicked four field goals and we won 12-9. The last field goal was for 44 yards in overtime. Fred Cox retired after the 1977 season, so that was only the second game of my career."

3. This most memorable moment belongs to which Viking?

"In 1965, in KEZAR Stadium in San Francisco, the Vikings trailed the 49ers 14-0 at the end of the first quarter and 35-14 at halftime. In the second half Fran Tarkenton was at his scrambling best and I was able to gain over 200 yards in receiving for the game and scored two touchdowns, the last of which was the winning score enabling the Vikings to win 42-41."

4. The highlight of this player's career with the Vikings was the opening game of 1970. In that game he directed the Vikes

Memorable Moments—Questions

to a 27-10 win over the Kansas City Chiefs, who only eight months earlier had defeated the Vikings in Super Bowl IV. Who was that quarterback?

5. A Vikings Hall of Fame defensive linemen once summed up his career this way: "There's the cliche that you play one game at a time. Well, I suppose I took that to the extreme and played one play at a time and tried to make every play the best play...You can't ride the highs and lows; you've got to perform at a high level all the time." With that statement in mind, who was the Vikings' defensive lineman whose response to the memorable moment question was the following?

"As I have indicated in the past, no particular moment, play, or game was more memorable than any other."

6. After many outstanding years as the quarterback of the New Orleans Saints, this player finished out his career with the Vikings. Who is the former Pro Bowl quarterback whose most memorable moment with the Vikings is the following?

"In 1984, during the last game of the season vs. Green Bay, for the second

Memorable Moments—Questions

time in three weeks at halftime I was told by head coach Les Steckel that I would play the second half. Both times we were down 31-0. I had a cracked tailbone and wasn't supposed to play. I wondered whether he wanted me to pull it out or just try to tie it up."

7. The most memorable moment for this running back was: "the 1969 divisional championship game against the L.A. Rams. This game was played on a cold, snowy Minnesota afternoon. It was the start of many great championship teams."

   Who was this Vikings player who scored two touchdowns?

8. When asked his most memorable moment, this Viking chose the team's first regular-season game which was also his first professional football game. On September 17, 1961, Minnesota beat the Chicago Bears 37-13, with this player coming off the bench to play a key role in the victory. Who is this Viking that went on to start and star in 170 more games for the team?

9. Which Vikings offensive end also picked this incredible September 17, 1961 victory over the Bears? As he states, his

Memorable Moments—Questions

most memorable moment was, "Our opening win against Chicago in the very first game of our franchise in 1961. I was able to help the team by catching some important passes."

This player caught three balls that day for 103 yards and one touchdown. He later went on to serve the Vikings as director of player personnel for nine years, and since 1975 he has held the post of director of football operations for the Vikings.

10. The most memorable moment for this Vikings defensive end was against the Pittsburgh Steelers on January 12, 1975.

"It was on my first play in Super Bowl IX (third play of the game) when I sacked Terry Bradshaw. He did surprise me when he got up."

11. Which Vikings punter, who played on successive Super Bowl teams, recalled the following big play?

"We were playing the Rams in an important midseason game in 1973, ahead by just one point, near the close of the game. I punted, and a running into the kicker penalty was called on the Rams. We kept the ball and eventually won the

Memorable Moments—Questions

game. Later that week I was given an "Oscar" by Merrill Swanson (team public relations director) for my acting job. Great week, and a fond memory."

12. Which Vikings tight end, who was dubbed "Chain Saw" by his teammates, said his most memorable moments were playing in Super Bowls VIII, IX, and XI? He further vividly remembers this 1975 playoff loss to Dallas because, as he says, "I think the 1975 Viking team was the best Viking team ever."

13. Which Vikings middle linebacker's most memorable moment was the following?

    "After growing up with a father who had gone to Stanford and had been a 49ers fan, I ultimately followed in the same tradition. Not only was I a 49ers fan, but John Brodie was my favorite player. My rookie year with the Vikings I got a chance to play against my hero in our last game of the season at Candlestick Park and "lo and behold" I even intercepted on of his passes! What a thrill it was!"

14. What all-pro Vikings defensive back chose the following as his memorable moment?

Memorable Moments—Questions

"It was in 1968 when we were in Philadelphia and had won the final game of the season. The whole team was on the bus outside the stadium listening to the radio to hear if the Packers beat the Bears so we could win the division for the first time." (The Packers did beat the Bears that day and the Vikes were the 1968 Central Division Champions.)

15. Which guard, who was a three-time Pro-Bowl selection for the Vikings (1975-77), will never forget the following?

    "It was at one of the championship games against the Rams. Here I am ready to run on the field for introductions, when Ron Yary grabs me and reminds me my jersey's on backwards."

16. Which player, who is the Vikings' second-leading career rusher, chose the following as the most memorable moment in his long and prolific career?

    "It was the Vikings vs. Rams at Metropolitan Stadium on December 27, 1969, for the Western Conference title. We were down at halftime and came back to win 23-20 with the help of our fans and a great effort from our team." (This victory was the Vikings' first postseason win.)

Memorable Moments—Questions

17. What defensive tackle, who played on the original 1961 Vikings and went on to serve as a cornerstone in the Vikings' emergence as the dominant force in the NFC in 1969-1971, chose the following?

    "My most memorable moment as a football player for the Vikings or any other team came during the 1969 season when we won the NFC Championship. The players, fans, coaches, and management all worked together in a degree of teamwork that was truly incredible. To me it was signfiicant of what can be accomplished by people working together toward a mutually determined and beneficial goal."

Memorable Moments
Answers

1. Ted Brown, 1979-1986

2. Rick Danmeier, 1977-1983

3. Paul Flatley, 1963-67

4. Gary Cuozzo, 1968-1971

5. Alan Page, 1967-1978

6. Archie Manning, 1983-84. (He completed 18 of 25 passes against the Packers.)

7. Dave Osborn, 1965-1975

Memorable Moments—Answers

8. 1986 Hall of Fame selection, Fran Tarkenton, 1961-66 and 1972-78

9. Jerry Reichow, 1961-64

10. Bob Lurtsema, 1972-76

11. Mike Eischeid, 1972-74

12. Stu Voigt, 1970-1980

13. Jeff Siemon, 1972-1982

14. Paul Krause, 1968-1979

15. Ed White, 1969-1977

16. Bill Brown, 1962-1974

17. Paul Dickson, 1961-1970